Distant but Loyal

Cranston's Italian Americans
Cranston, Rhode Island / Itri, Italy

Two Cities in Time

Anne T. Romano, Ph.D.

Portland • Oregon
INKWATERPRESS.COM

ISBN-10 1-59299-303-6
ISBN-13 978-1-59299-303-1

Publisher: Inkwater Press

Printed in the U.S.A.
All paper is acid free and meets the ANSI standards for archival quality paper

Dedicated to
My Aunt Zia Italia Fabrizio Sinapi
In gratitude for all of her songs, stories, memories
and love that made this work possible

CHAPTERS

INDEX OF PHOTOGRAPHY

INTRODUCTION

The wedding of Nadia Chiusano and Nando Capotosto on August 12, 1999 in the village of Itri, Italy (population 6,219) went unnoticed in Rome and Palermo, and barely got a mention in the towns near the tiny Italian village where they were born. But it was big news that summer in the village of Knightsville in Cranston, Rhode Island, U.S.A. (population 8,000).

"Tanti Auguri di Felicita Perenne", exclaimed Salvatore DeLuca, a Cranston resident for 25 years. "Lo figlio di Antonio Capotosto si sposato! Per cento anni!" he exclaimed to family and friends.

When Itri's residents have an announcement about weddings or births or any of the other news of interest, they often fax, telephone or e-mail it to Cranston, where, chances are, interest will be just as high as at home. Cranston has the reputation of being "The Most Italian of All American Cities." Proportionally, Cranston is the home of the highest amount of Italian-Americans. Totaling 38% it is greater than any other settlement of Italian Americans in the United States. This intensity is due to one group of Italians, the Itrani, who left a small village in Italy and settled in Knightsville. Of Knightsville's 8,000 residents, 85% are of Italian ancestry and 65% of those of those are Itrani. There are 3,000 miles of land and ocean that separate that village in Italy and the city of Cranston in the state of Rhode Island, U.S.A. Yet, there is a link between the two villages that defies this distance. A tie that began with the first Itrani who left Itri for the new world and continues until today with residents at both ends maintaining connections with each other. There have been many communities in the United States that have attracted Italian immigrants. Knightsville may be the only one formed however, when almost an entire Italian town, Itri, located on the Appian Way, midway between Rome and Naples, transported itself to a new land, while purposely setting about to preserve the traditions and way of life of the old land.

How did this tie develop between these two disparate places? The answer is twofold; the patterns of emigration and the endurance of tradition. As of emigration, over the past half-century or more, about as many people have left the village of Itri and moved to Cranston as live there now. Practically everyone in Itri has at least one relative or friend living in Cranston.

The emigrants from Itri centered themselves in a particular section of Cranston, called Knightsville. Today, grandparents, uncles, aunts, cousins still live within blocks of one another in Knightsville, although some have ventured to the outer limits of the city and beyond. As for the strength of tradition, every year the Rector of the Maria SS Della Civita Santuary travels from the mountains, vineyards, olive groves and pear arbors of Itri to visit the Itri diaspora in Cranston and be part of a tradition. And in that context, the residents of Cranston swell the population of Itri every summer in an annual return to celebrate the same tradition. That tradition occurring simultaneously in both countries during the third week of July is the annual festival honoring Maria Santissima della Civita known as Saint Mary in the United States, and in Italy, La Madonna della Civita—patron saint of Itri.

In 1996 I personally came face to face with the strength of that tradition. That year I succumbed to an annual rite in my family. Annually, beginning in May my father would begin to reminisce about his early days in Knightsville and long to return for _La Festa_. Through all of my growing years I had been hearing about "the feast in Knightsville" and of course La Madonna who had a place of honor in our home, but I had never been to the feast. Also, throughout my life I listened to stories of my father emigrating from Itri to Knightsville at the young age of 15, having been "called" by his older sister and shortly thereafter leaving to find a better life in New York City. There's a right time for everything in life and that year seemed to be the right time to satisfy my father's wishes to return to Cranston. My father was then 91 years old—if not now, when? The trip was a rewarding one for many reasons. Primarily, I got to please my aging father's desire to not only celebrate the most important feast day of his culture, but to also renew contacts with "paisani"—those kin and honorary kin—who emigrated from the same village in Italy. On a personal note, I also finally found my roots. I discovered a connection, links with other descendants from a similar but distant culture. For the first time in my life I met another "DeLuca." As a child growing up on the streets of New York City, I can remember wondering if I would ever meet another person with the same last name as mine. Living without benefit of an extended family, my parents and brothers were the only DeLuca's I knew. And I never did meet any other DeLuca's throughout my grade school years, high school years and years working in Manhattan. It wasn't until many years later; when I brought my father to Cranston did I see my family name advertising area businesses and professional services. Although there was no known blood relationship, I still felt a sense of pride at seeing my family name and making that connection. Finally, I had the opportunity to meet other DeLuca's and uncover my link with the past and possibly open doors to the future.

What I also found in Knightsville was the traditional comforts and protection that comes with membership in an ethnic group within a community; something that had been absent from my life growing up in heterogeneous New York City. The sense of belonging and feelings of reassurance that allow you to make Sunday morning visits—never having to ring a doorbell—seeing parents, sisters, cousins and old friends. These visits seem to be a reminder that there is one place in the world where you unquestionably belonged and were accepted. I learned about the unity of family life, the meaning of blood ties and memory, and ethnic pride. I also had the heart-warming pleasure of witnessing a profoundly sensitive respect for the elderly that existed in Cranston. As word got around town that "Giacinto DeLuca from New York" (my father) has arrived for the feast, the residents of Cranston made sure to pay their respects to my father, taking the time to visit with him, marveling to him how wonderful he looked and wishing him well. In addition, during the processional march through the streets of Cranston, the men carrying the 1,500 pound statue of La Madonna during a very-hot July day, stopped the processional and lowered the statue close to my father sitting in a wheelchair along the parade route, so that he might touch the statue and bless himself. It was as though he were royalty.

The Itrani's have a reputation for hospitality that defies international distance. "The door is always open" and "There is always enough for one more" are household expressions. Travelers to Italy are always received courteously and graciously and this general behavior has survived in America. A visitor to the home of an Itrani is always offered a drink of cordial, brandy or vermouth. Usually this is followed with a pastry and a cup of espresso. If it is close to mealtime, the visitor is always invited to participate without ceremony. The host is insulted if the offer is not accepted. And this hospitality is not only demonstrated during the time of the feast but at all times throughout the year.

Encouraged by the warmth and hospitality of the Itrani during my first visit, I decided to proceed further to examine other facets of this wonderful community of Itrani's. What were the lives of the Itrani like? How did their lives differ from mine? How different would my life have been had my father stayed in Cranston instead of moving to New York City? It is said that wherever you are reared, marks you for life. Being an outsider, growing up as a child of Italian immigrants in a mixed neighborhood in Manhattan, I learned very quickly how to be an American. That meant adapting the American way in language and in attitude as well as unfortunately, distance from my culture. How different would my life have been had I spent my formative years in homogeneous Cranston?

Knightsville, a relatively small segment of the larger Cranston region has a history which bears some commonality with other Italian American communities in the United States. Many of these communities emerged in the later 1800s and in the early twentieth century as immigrants left their villages in southern Italy to begin new lives in a new land. Similarly, Knightsville's beginnings as an Italian-American community dates back to the last decade of the nineteenth century when immigrants from Itri began moving in. Over the next century Cranston emerged as the prime Italian-American community of Rhode Island. There have been numerous statistical analyses as well as historical studies of immigrants in the new world. Taken together, these publications represent an invaluable contribution to our understanding of the process of migration and indicate that the process of assimilation in America has varied for the different immigrant groups. Nearly every group at first established some sort of ethnic community: Scandinavians in the Midwest, Chinese and Japanese in California, Mexicans in the Southwest and the Italians primarily in New York City. New York City, with the largest Italian community in the United States was the center of immigrant research. Accordingly, these studies have reinforced negative tales of settlement patterns in crowded ghettos, complete with accounts of crime, poverty, poor health and exploitation.

The effects of this preoccupation with the negative aspects of Italian immigration, has been the acceptance of these findings as representative of the entire Italian culture and experience. It was assumed that life that characterized the Italian urban experience could readily be applied to all Italian enclaves. This assumption had the unfortunate result of neglecting alternate Italian immigration lifestyles that might have challenged the traditional picture of the Italian immigrant in America.

The pages that follow vividly illustrate the impact of a different environment on Italian immigrants. It tells of the Italian foreign-born who did migrate to America and suffered less discrimination, were readily assimilated, and honestly competed with current residents in their rapid rise to wealth and power. In doing so, a new image emerges bearing little resemblance to stereotypes that have been present for generations. Proud Italian mill-workers and farm-workers, rather than exploited sweat-shop laborers; community concern and acceptance rather than rejection and degradation; a sense of belonging rather than isolation; one-family homes and not slums and congested tenements; vegetable gardens rather than pushcarts in the street; honest, hard-working people contributing to the economy rather than crime; respectful children rather than delinquents; and economic success rather than the devastating effects of the city handout- the welfare system. We have all been bombarded with media stereotypes of Italian immigration. In presenting this new image, old interpretations of the past that have distorted the image of the Italian immigrant, and become stereotypes that have lasted for a generation, must be rethought and discarded.

The emphasis throughout this book is on the connections between Itri in Italy and Cranston in Rhode Island, and on the fact that for the Itrani both places were significant and continue to be important even to this day. Three related sets of questions shaped this book. The first question concerns the economic, social, and physical conditions that existed in both countries which encouraged migration. Frequently referred to as the push-pull theory of emigration it reflected the need in the United

States for workers following the industrial revolution and the poor, disintegrating conditions in Italy. Push factors sometimes begin the process, for example, the rural poverty that makes villagers dissatisfied with their lives. A common "pull" factor is the attraction of the larger city where opportunity is thought to be greater. The second question might be; why did some choose to flee rather than stay and make changes? In Itri as well as Cranston, it was discovered, out-migration was built on a surprising foundation, the family and informal social networks. Sometimes referred to as chain-migration, the process involved the "calling" of a relative with assurances of a job in America. The metaphor of chain migration has been used to emphasize the extent to which village solidarity determined emigrant destination. It is regarded as the most important influence of immigrants' choice of an American destination.

A key to the life of Italian community life in America is an understanding of the phenomenon known as campanilismo. The word campanilismo derives from the word campana (bell) and campanile (church tower) referring to the view of the world that includes reluctance to extend social, cultural, and economic contacts beyond points from which the village bell would still be heard. It assumes solidarity among those who heard the ringing of the same church bell. This village solidarity allowed migrants to cooperate in forging migration chains. To put it simply, migrants followed people they knew and trusted—their neighbors who had migrated earlier and established a transplanted village in some U.S. city. First described by the post World War II generation of Australian scholars (MacDonald and MacDonald, 1964) the concept refers to personal relationships among family, friends and paesani in both the sending and receiving communities which influenced destination, settlement, occupations, mobility and social interacting (see also, MacDonald and MacDonald, 1970; Price 1963; Baily, 1982). Many followed this traditional pattern in which a single adventurer went ahead, found work, and alerted other workers from the same village. Immigrants used interpersonal networks to form chains of migration that enabled them to resettle in paesani colonies.

The immigrant deciding to emigrate followed a specific route. He would go to a specific town in the New World, live in a particular area of the city, and join a specific mutual aid society. In addition, he most likely traveled with his paesani and relying on recommendations from friends, would go directly to living quarters where only their paesani lived. Often an immigrant and his family would open their house to boarders, almost invariably men from their own paese who were in America temporarily. The Boarding House continued the maintenance of regional ties since all of the boarders came from the same village. They also assured the survival of traditional culture, including the foods as prepared by the women of the houses. Their jobs, usually arranged through padroni, would be most likely in certain establishments where his fellow paesani already worked. And, he would most likely marry a woman from his home town or social group.

Thus, in the heart of most American cities one could find in the Italian neighborhoods, a Sicilian, a Calabrian, a Neapolitan, an Abruzzian enclave, all within a few blocks, and each with its specific traditions, manner of living, and dialect. Most Italian colonies were actually groupings of immigrants from the same region or village. In New York City during the 1890s, people from specific regions tended to settle in specific neighborhoods; Neapolitans in Mulberry Bend, Genoese on Baxter Street, and Sicilians between Houston and Spring Streets. Years later, a similar phenomenon was noted in Greenwich Village, where immigrants from the same town tended to move into the same tenement. Other American cities with regionally identifiable Italian neighborhoods were; the Abruzzi in Pittsburgh's Panther Hollow district and Sicilians from four villages (Santo Stefano Quisquina, Alessandria della Rocca, Cianciniana, and Contessa Entellina) comprised the Italian-American community in Tampa, Florida.

Smaller cities and towns were settled by immigrants from a single province or community. For example, Roseto, Pennsylvania was settled almost entirely by immigrants from Roseto Valfortore, in Apulia. Rillton, in Pennsylvania attracted a substantial number of immigrants from the Piedmontese village of Monteu de Po. Galveston, Texas has an Italian-American fishing community composed almost entirely of immigrants from a village near Catania, Sicily.

Although not precisely representative, Knightsville shares a similar history and is characterized by the intra-ethnic social and cultural patterns found in many Italian-American populations living in other urban and suburban communities of the United States.

Critics of the ethnic enclave see them as refuges, islands within the larger community which ensured the newly arrived immigrant a sense of protection and a social life slowing their assimilation to the new country's ways. But a major fear on the part of the immigrant was that the assimilation process would lead to loss of the mother tongue and of precious cultural heritage. However, as we have seen in recent ethnic studies and particularly will see in Knightsville, the sense of ethnicity is still strong with subsequent generations hanging on to old-world ways.

A third question regards the effects of chain migration and the social and physical conditions of immigration on the Itrani. Were these immigrants a distinctive subculture, self-selected as they appeared to reject and severe ties to their homeland? Did out-migration facilitate or serve to undermine the transplantation of rural tradition to the United States. Which traditions survived the transport? And what was the impact of the American environment on transplantation?

The organization of this book follows these three sets of questions about the past relationships and continuing relationship between Itri and Cranston. The first chapter offers an overview of social conditions, economic change, peasant life, international migration, and working conditions that were the catalyst for migration out of Itri. The second chapter continues the story of Itri in the United States. It examines the conditions of change as they prevail in a rapidly developing nation and more specifically in Cranston, Rhode Island. Cranston is said to be the most Italian of all American cities since proportionally Italian Americans total 38% of the population. This chapter addresses the question; why have so many Italians settled in Rhode Island? How did this growth occur? It also examines the importance of occupation in shaping the settlement of Itrani in Knightsville.

The important role that religion plays for the Itrani is addressed in chapter 3. The Itrani feel they are a chosen people because the Madonna chose to be among them. Thus, they feel able to call upon the Madonna for help in times of need and experience a sense of protection. This belief in her miraculous powers remains constant throughout the lifetime of the Itrani, and is a unifying force in the community. The annual feast as it was first celebrated in Knightsville and as it continues today is described in this chapter.

Chapter 4 introduces us to some notables from Itri and its vicinity. Most people will remember the film "Two Women" for which the Italian actress Sophia Loren won an Academy Award, but not know that the movie was filmed in the hills of Itri. Another notable from Itri was the infamous "Fra Diavolo", whose history is chronicled in this chapter.

Chapter 5 provides us with some insight to the Itrani via community folklore, their proverbs and folk songs and their use of the "Sopranommo" a common practice in small communities. We are also offered a rare insight into an Itrani Wedding which was recorded for history and transcribed therein.

In recent years we have heard much of global interdependence; a state in which the lives of people in different parts of the world are intertwined closely. In this era of instant communication—cellular phones, fax machines, personal computer, the internet—information into and out of countries is made easier. In this era of improved transportation and reduced costs, travel in and out of countries is also much easier. Since 1980 the United States has become part of a more interdependent, more competitive economic order, a world economy. The current level of global interdependence and competition reflects a multitude of interactions between Americans and other cultures. Although American sociologists and anthropologists have written about culture for more than 100 years, only in the last decade have non-academics (particularly business persons) taken an interest in culture with the understanding that knowledge about other cultures will help negotiate deals and sell products to foreign consumers.

Italian society also has undergone an impressive process of change in the last 40 years. Italy has changed from a mostly agricultural economy into a highly industrialized one; millions of people moved from the South to the North and from the countryside to the cities changing patterns of social behavior and interactions. A new Italian society has emerged. The modernization of the economy has profoundly changed the way of life of the Italians, whose standards are today comparable to those of any major industrialized democracy in the world.

Indeed, relations between Itri and Cranston over the years have been a two-way relationship, thriving on a mutual give and take while enhancing a solid partnership. We can expect that this partnership will continue to grow in a more global, interdependent way.

Prevalent economic conditions in Italy that led to the great emigration were some of the darkest chapters of Italy's history. From that time of pain and grief, Italy and the United States were to forge unbreakable bonds that have continued to this day. In the years that followed, millions of Italians made a lonely journey across the Atlantic in search of a new life. They remained in America to work in its factories, to build its towns and railways, and to play their full part in its local communities. They found here a home away from home.

For the Italian American interested in gleaning insight into the generations of nineteenth century Italians in America who made a special impact on their adopted land, the story of the migration of the Itrani is truly remarkable. They identified strongly with their ethnic roots while making a memorable contribution to their new country. The dedication and contributions of the Itrani stand as a testimony to their love and devotion to the United States which in turn deserves the commendation of all Americans.

The beginning of a new millennium presents an opportunity to evaluate the past, and seek new directions and dreams. It is a time of special promise and opportunity. The close and enduring bonds between Italy and the United States remains as strong as ever, but it has also taken new shape and form as part of the wider interdependent relationship between Europe and the United States. We all feel an enormous pride in the role played by millions of Italian men and women in the building of America over the years.

The contributions of the Itrani are an enduring part of that legacy.

My debt to the Itrani is inestimable. Visiting them and being part of their lives exposed me to many enriching experiences. During the years since I first began to write this book, I have become indebted to many individuals and institutions. As in the past, the Enrico Fermi Library in Bronx, New York has proved to be an invaluable resource. In addition, the Rhode Island Historical Society, The Cranston and Knightsville Libraries, the Cranston Historical Society, and the Libraries in and around Itri, Italy have been most helpful. Various colleagues and friends and relatives have provided insights and aid to this project. I would like to express my sincere gratitude and love to Zia Italia Fabrizio Sinapi for sharing thoughts, stories, songs, information and memories during our many visits. My thanks to Kathleen Daley for providing a quiet place in her Southampton, Long Island home so that I might complete this book. Thank you to Kathleen Daley and Andi Wolos for their very talented work assembling the graphics for this book. Much gratitude to the Itrani in Knightsville, especially Salvatore Mancini and Tony Canella for sharing their work with me and Deacon Peter A. Ceprano of Saint Mary's Church. And to my cousins Salvatore and Agnese DeLuca and family and extended family for their gracious hospitality.

AUTHOR AND FRIENDS ON FIRST VISIT TO ITRI-1952

CHAPTER 1

IMMIGRANTS CONGREGATE IN CRANSTON BUT LEAVE THEIR HEARTS IN ITRI

In the heart of Knightsville, a village in west Cranston Rhode Island, there is a commemorative plaque embedded in the ground on which a map of Itri is carved. In 1967, the city of Cranston in recognition of the contribution of all the Itrani immigrants dedicated a monument. To further honor these immigrants, this section of Knightsville became thereafter known as "Piazza Itri". As the result of changes in the city's construction, the monument was relocated. In July, 1988, on the occasion of the annual feast in honor of "Maria Santissima Della Civita" a new memorial was dedicated to the Itrani immigrants and erected in "Itri Memorial Square." In the words of the President of St. Mary's Feast Society:

> "The granite stone memorial serves as an everlasting monument and a reminder to future generations of the achievements of the Itrani people, their love of God, their love of the Blessed Mother under the title of Maria Santissima Della Civita, and the love of their family which as made them a proud and giving people. They have had a tremendous impact on our community that will last for generations."(St. Mary's Feast Society, July 1988)

The granite stone memorial is emblazoned with the words *"ITRI SQUARE."* On the ground in front of the memorial, a circular plaque set in bricks bear's information concerning the dedication ceremony. More importantly this concrete wall contains the names of the 64 original immigrants from Itri who founded the Knightsville Italian American community: Cardi, Del Bonis, DeLuca, DiPrete, Maggiacomo, Sinapi, LaRocca, Manzi, Ruggieri, Mancini, Saccoccia, Paparelli, and Fabrizio. DelBova, DiBiase, Guglietta.....

These families were some of the first of many millions who left their native Italy, to live in, to work in, and to help build the city of Cranston.

ITRI MEMORIAL SQUARE IN KNIGHTSVILLE

This exceptional commemorative to the first families of Cranston, fashioned from the most durable of products, serves as an indelible reminder of their contributions. Observing this memorial raises several questions. Who are these people?; Why did they leave their families, their friends, their country, to emigrate to an unfamiliar land?; And why to Cranston? What did they do in America?' What were their lives like in Itri? How did they live? How did their lives change in America? Where are they now?; and finally, was it all worth it, after all?

In order to understand fully the significance of their emigration it is necessary to return to the source, Itri, and make a brief examination of the social and historical environment from which it developed. This environment imprinted certain characteristics on their emigration so strongly, that they have endured through the years and have been passed on to subsequent generations.

ITALY: THE LAND AND ITS PEOPLE

The country of Italy has clear natural boundaries—mountains in the north and encircling seas in the rest of the country. These natural boundaries separate Italy from her neighbors in Europe and the Mediterranean. The country stretches in a northwest-south-easterly direction for about eight hundred miles—approximately the distance between northern Maine and the southernmost tip of North Carolina. The climate of Italy is more temperate than it is in most areas of America at corresponding latitudes. Although it is hot everywhere in the summer, and the winters can be very cold in the north, the country does not experience the extremes with which America is familiar. Italy consists of a long peninsula that bisects the Mediterranean into an eastern and a western basin, two major islands—Sicily and Sardinia (three with Corsica, the French island that geographically is part of Italy)—dozens of smaller islands (eighteen of them are in the Tuscan archipelago between the Tyrrhenian and the Ligurian seas, and the Aeolian and Aegades archipelagoes north and west of Sicily), and a large continental area in the north, bounded from east to west by Yugoslavia, Austria, Switzerland, and France.

In area, Italy is slightly larger than Arizona, that is to say, about one-thirtieth the size of the continental United States.

THE PENINSULAR REGIONS

The peninsula accounts for over two-fifths of Italy. Since early in the third century B.C., an irregular line running from the mouth of the Rubicon in the east to the

MAP OF ITALY WITH AREA OF ITRI NOTED

mouth of the Magra in the west, along the Apennine watershed between Tuscany and Emilia—Romagna, has marked the boundary between peninsular and continental Italy. Except for a few small plains—most of them along the coast or inland in the valleys of the Tiber and Arno, the peninsula is mountainous or hilly. Its backbone is the Apennine Range, which begins at the Passo di Giovi in continental Italy and continues beyond the peninsula in the mountain ranges of northern Sicily. The highest peak, the Gran Sasso d'Italia (the Great Rock of Italy), reaches over nine thousand feet. Much of the range has been barren since ancient times, but woods and forests can still be found from Aspromonte in the south to Abetone in the north, and a good deal of valuable reforestation has taken place in recent decades.

Rivers are numerous, but most have little water and many dry up completely in the summer months. Lakes are few, fewer than in ancient times. The largest of all was Lake Ficino fifty miles east of Rome in the center of mountainous Marsica. Emptied of its water in the nineteenth century by a tunnel dug through the mountains, Fucino has been trans-formed into fertile farmland. The miniscule Lake of Averno near Naples was in pre-Christian times credited with being the entrance to hell.

Mountains and hills divide the peninsula into separate and varied districts where in the past communities tended to develop along divergent lines. Although people move and mingle today as never before, customs and dialects still vary greatly from one district to another, as does the appearance of cities and villages. In the course of centuries some districts have changed their names and the boundaries of all the districts have shifted somewhat. Thus, the result of the agelong historical process has been the division of the peninsula into ten districts known as provinces, each with its distinctive way of life.

Latium, the province to which the town of Itri belongs, is a little smaller than Massachusetts and the heart of the peninsula and of all Italy. Thirty centuries ago Latium was the name of a small district on the left bank of the lower Tiber, inhabited by communities of the Latin tribe. Today, Latium in South Central Italy-stretches along the Tyrrhenian Sea north and south of the Tiber, and inland as far as the Apennines.

In ancient times Latium supported a considerable population, but over the years the soil became exhausted, the water, no longer drained, stagnated, and malaria developed killing residents in the low-lying areas. One hundred years ago, much of the area surrounding Rome (Latium's one large city then as now) was a wasteland. This is no longer so. The Campagna di Roma, the Maremma to the north, and the Pontine Marshes to the south have all been reclaimed. Malaria has disappeared. Roads have once again opened the countryside, now dotted within villages and farmhouses. For Italians, Latium means Rome—not always Italy's political capital, but since the third century BC, Italy's chief city. Rome is more to Italy than Paris is to France or London to England; not only is it the seat of government, the political capital, and the spiritual center and headquarters of Roman Catholicism; it is an idea, a meaningful symbol of past glories and the future promise. Rome grew to unify Italy and later to rule the Mediterranean world of which it was the largest metropolis. It is said to have numbered up to two million inhabitants in ancient times after which came long, lean years. Magnificent buildings—palaces, courts of law, temples, theatres—decayed, many disappeared completely; rubble filled the streets, shepherds led their herd and flock to pasture amid the ruins. The population at times shrank to a few tens of thousands. Nevertheless, sections of the city continued to live, and more important, the idea of Rome never died—it scarcely weakened. Today, with nearly three million people, Rome is Italy's largest city.

ITRI

Itri is a gracious little city located in this region of Italy, along the coast south of Rome. Its territory extends along the Appian Way, the main thoroughfare to the south. This delightful city was inhabited by various people, even in pre-historic times. Later it became part of the Roman Empire. The Romans left their indelible marks on Itri. It was during the Roman domination that the Appian Way was constructed making Itri a very important part of Rome's expansion plans. Because of the importance of its strategic location as a line to the south, Itri played a major role during the glorious period of the Roman Empire for commerce and travel. It was not until after the medieval period that its population grew to any significant size. Strong urban explosion took place around the now famous "Castle of Itri" and the primitive tower. The "Medieval Center," was at that time surrounded by a high stone wall with towers and gates that served as protection against invasion. Thus, noteworthy medieval monuments including the famous Castle of Itri and several churches of S. Maria Anunziata still stand today.

GIOACCHINO MURAT FOUNTAIN IN CENTER OF ITRI (1811-1812)

Throughout the centuries, Itri witnessed the transit of the legions of Rome and Hannibal, and withstood the influx of Vandals, Goths, and Huns. It survived the campaigns of Justinian's armies, Norman raiders, Crusaders and Saracens, Hoenstaufens, Angevins, Popes, Bourbons, and Austrians, as well as assorted bandits and pirates. In later years during World War II, the Germans occupied Itri. In a 1993 interview for Yankee Magazine, Domenico Troccoli who was born in Itri vividly recalled the horrors of that war. He stated:

AUTHOR WITH GRANDMOTHER IN FRONT OF MURAT FOUNTAIN -1952

"In 1943 we went into the mountains to hide. Not because of the Germans, but because the Allied bombing destroyed 75 percent of Itri. We stayed there nine months. We ate grass, we ate horse. In 1944 the Americans came. We came out of the mountains. Then they took me prisoner thinking I was a Fascisti."

ANCIENT CASTLE OVERLOOKING ITRI (882 A.D.)

During World War II, seventy-five percent of Itri's buildings were destroyed by 54 Allied bombings, as the Germans were driven out during the battle of Monte Cassino. In addition to the heavy casualties sustained as a result of the Allied Bombardment, the Germans executed several Itrani as hostages as they retreated before the Allied forces. Liberation of Itri by the Americans did not spell the end to the wartime suffering, however, since the Americans were soon replaced by a contingent of soldiers from Morocco, Algiers, and the French Sudan who occupied Itri under the command of Marshal Juin. During their occupation of Itri, they plundered the village and committed wholesale rape.

Upon the end of the fighting, a massive reconstruction effort was begun. The reconstruction project was quite successful. Very few traces of wartime damage remain. The wartime destruction also initiated another wave of emigration from Itri. Many of these emigrants would find their way to Knightsville, as had their predecessors, where they would experience a relatively easy transition to American life.

Itri is an agricultural and commercial center which borders with Fondi, Campodimele to its north, Formia and Gaeta to its east, Sperlonga to its west. Fondi, located along the Appian Way was situated along the major trade route from Rome to the Port of Brindin. Fondi was once part of the Kingdom of Naples. The malaria epi-

COUSIN LORETA WITH DAILY HARVEST FROM HER FRUIT FARM IN FONDI PREPARING FOR MARKET

demic of 1633 which was caused by the use of stagnant water after a severe drought reduced the general population of Fondi from 10,000 to 332. In a short time, the city of Fondi became a deserted moor. Itri is also located less than one mile to the south of the Tyrrhenian Sea. In the 1971 census, nearly 7,000 Itrani inhabited this historical village.

In appearance, central Itri has not changed significantly in its long history. It retains the look and feel of a medieval fortress town, with its ancient houses, narrow streets, arched gateways, and winding alleys. According to history, the original inhabitants of Itri were descended from Greeks who had settled the coastal town of Amlycla. Followers of the teachings of Pythagoras, they were forbidden to kill animals. When their city became infested with serpents, they fled to the mountains and established a new city, Itri.

Its eastern point, Gaeta is a beautiful coastal vacation and bathing resort and an active boating and fishing port. A handsome fortress of ancient origin, but transformed from the 13th to the 16th century, it sits on a promontory jutting into the sea in this town. A 12th century cathedral is also an interesting site, but visitors to Gaeta enjoy a stroll through the bazaar-like, narrow alleys parallel to the Lungomare Caboto. The pleasure yachts anchored in the basin are quite posh. Gaeta-Itri is also well known to this day for top quality olives and olive oil. To this

AUTHOR WITH DAUGHTER ANNETTE ON ITRI STREET OF GRANDPARENTS HOME
LAUNDRY DRYING IN WINDOW OF ITRI HOME

day, every April in Itri, there is a festival celebrating the olive harvest, "La Feste Gli'Olivi".

The coast between Gaeta and Formia was a favorite resort of ancient Romans. Gaeta was a prosperous duchy from 9th to 12th Centuries, when it fell to Normans and later to the kingdom of Naples. Its port and citadel were strongly fortified by the Bourbons. The ancient greatness that there was, under the Greeks, and the medieval greatness that existed under the Norman rule declined during Spaniard and Bourbon rule. Neglect, weakness, and oppression in varying degrees characterized the rulers. There was no government which the people could call their own. The defeat in Gaeta of the Bourbons after a long siege (1860-1861) by Italian troops marked the end of their Kingdom. Later, Gaeta as well as other parts of Itri suffered heavy damage from air and naval bombings (1943-1944) during the Second World War damaging the land itself including cathedrals and other medieval buildings.

Gaeta is the site of one of the Itrani's most interesting legends. Il Santuario della Montagna Spaccata, (The Sanctuary of the Split

Mountain) is located in Gaeta. The church is located alongside a narrow corridor which divides two separate but perfectly fitted mountains; the bumps and grooves of one mountain fit perfectly into the grooves and bumps of the other side of the narrow corridor. To the left of the Church, along the path which now contains one of the strongest symbols of Catholicism, the Stations of the Cross, one notices "La Mano del Turco," an imprint of a hand into the mountainside. According to this ancient legend of "La Montagna Spaccata", while Jesus Christ was dying on the cross, the painful screams of his mother, the Blessed Virgin Mary were of such strength that three mountains split in half. It is said that the split was so perfect that not a single stone fell to the ground. A Turkish sailor viewing the splitting of the mountain sarcastically doubted that it was a real mountain and proclaimed that they must be made of ricotta cheese. Wanting to prove that the consistency of the mountain was indeed ricotta cheese, he reached into the mountain to get a taste, thus, leaving an imprint of his hand in the side of the mountain. Accordingly, this site has been credited with several miracles.

Sperlonga, to the west of Itri is perhaps Lazio's (the modern name for the region of Latium) loveliest summer resort. This whitewashed town has a Moorish look. About a half-mile south of the town is a small, but fascinating "Museo Nazionale Archeologico di Sperlonga." Within this museum there are displays of works uncovered during excavation of a seaside estate believed to have been owned by the Emperor Tiberius. Among the finds are the fragments of a larger-than-life marble Cyclops Polyphemus being attacked by Odysseus (Ulysses to the Romans). This masterpiece was found within the Grotto of Tiberius. A few miles away from the museum is the actual

THE SPLIT MOUNTAIN "LA MONTAGNA SPACCATA" IN GAETA

ARCHEOLOGICAL MUSEUM IN SPERLONGA-STATUE FROM TIBERIUS'S CAVE

Grotto di Tiberio, a great cave on the beach where the emperor Tiberius maintained a huge marine theater. Various ancient statues were found in the cave, and some can still be seen there.

Itrani have speculated for years on the origin of the name of their beloved land. One explanation is that it is a derivative on the Latin word—Iter—which means road, passage or street. Since Itri was a sort of passageway from North to South this seems to be a likely explanation. Ancient Roman inscriptions on the walls of Itri support this theory. Another, that Itri was derived from – I Tre – one of three.

WHY LEAVE?

Certainly, one of the most compelling and perplexing questions is: Why did so many leave this beautiful land, with a heritage of

ITRI COAT OF ARMS

some of the great artisans of the world? There have been many reasons offered in the literature studying the outflow of southern Italians from their homeland. They are: cheapened, rapid ocean transportation—the result of technological progress (By 1870's steamships crossed the Atlantic in ten days;) the instigations of agents of steamship companies—(the padrone system); the spirit of adventure—those who ventured forth were explorers of sort; and although it is true that many Italian immigrants just happen to come upon steamship tickets which were purchased in the United States, it cannot be said that they were the sole cause. The most conspicuous difference between the regions from which emigration proceeded and the countries of immigration is economic. The causes which have sustained an emigration of millions of people for half a century do in truth constitute a defect or an inadequacy of great magnitude in the Italian economic system. The emigration out of Italy is essentially the final outcome of a chain of causes reaching well into the past, and as such, is a notable historic phenomenon. A century before Christ, Rome was already the first Mediterranean power. The history of the Italian people is steeped in the richness of a lengthly past. From her days of antiquity through the Renaissance Italy's history created the unique memory of a proud and powerful heritage never quite erased from the Italian consciousness. For the inhabitants of Italy, however this sense of glory receded as the country approached modern times.

Before the Risorgimento brought Italy unification, she was plagued by foreign armies tramping over her countryside. Throughout much of the nineteenth century, Italy was at the mercy of a reactionary Austria or an invading France. Southern Italy had experienced more than two millenia of foreign rule that is two thousand years of various forms of political and economic oppression. From the eighteenth to the twentieth centuries, other physical conditions on the Italian peninsula encouraged the departure of hundreds of thousands of persons. For centuries, Italy's peasants struggled with a parched, stubborn, and eroded land. Poor rainfall, lessened by the many high mountains reduced the tillable acreage. Small peasant village farms had topsoil drained away by centuries of erosion. Scorched and sandy plots of terrain, perennially lacking in water made the growing of crops at best marginal. Except for Portugal, no country in Europe had a lower consumption of meat per inhabitant. In some of Italy's provinces the peasant diet consisted of little more than bread and water with macaroni available a few times a week and meat only once in a while. In addition, Italy suffered from physical hardships, among them; droughts, floods, malaria, depleted soil and mineral resources and a series of earthquakes. In Calabria alone there were earthquakes in 1854, 1870, 1894, 1905, 1907 and the worse of all in 1980, leaving a legacy of destruction of life and property. The houses of the contadini are small and simple, often a shed without windows or chimney. Stone, brick and mud were the materials of composition. Washing facilities are meager, drainage is absent with indoor plumbing non-existent. Oil or petroleum may be burned, but many a family had its evening meal in darkness. The house itself, often of only one room, may contain during the night and part of the day, not only the entire family with a demoralizing collapse of privacy, but the goat, poultry, and other animals of the family. With the work place far away, those working may remain in the fields overnight or longer depending on the season, resting on the ground, or on straw, with a straw roof over his head. The overwhelming majority of Itrani as high as ninety-six or ninety-seven percent remained peasants, people without any power in their remote villages, repeating the same cycle of life as the generations that had preceded them.

With the unification of Italy in 1870, there wasn't much change. Land, the very basis of contidini survival, grew increasingly scarcer as escalating taxes forced many of the peasants to sell their land. At that time Italy was divided into three main levels of class structure. At the top were a small number of powerful landlords who comprised some one or two percent of the population and owned a good deal of the best land. These were often absentee landlords who lived in the cities and delegated responsibilities to the land agents. Secondly, a group of bureaucrats and professional people who were less than ten percent of the population and catered to the needs of the elite classes. Finally, were the vast majority of the peasants who lived in economic depression. Most of the latter owned no land and hired themselves on a daily basis to work the field of others. The level of wages was low for the mezzagiorne peasant worker. In 1905, the average wages per day in the Provence of Latium was: Men, forty cents (.40) per day. The highest summer earnings on a monthly basis were expected to be $17.50 to $19.05. In the United States, the wages were considerably higher. Consider the following posted sign, seeking workers for the Croton Reservoir construction:

LABORERS NEEDED FOR HIRE:

Common laborer—white $1.30-$1.50
Common laborer—colored $1.25-$1.40
Common laborer—Italian $1.15-$1.25
(Public Notice at New York's Croton Reservoir, 1895)

• •

These are the conditions that the immigrant left behind him. Needless to say these conditions shaped the Italian-American character. The Italians who came to America expected improvement and searched for opportunity. They were achievement oriented. Having endured deprivation, they fully expected to and wanted to work hard. In America, they expected their hard work to result in an improved economic and social position. They had no difficulty in adapting to the work ethic in America. People do not cross continents and oceans without considerable thought. Nor do they uproot themselves from family, friends, and familiar terrain without significant strain. The motivation to emigrate must be overwhelming before the fateful step is taken.

Thus, with few exceptions the immigrants flocked to America for economic reasons, as Alberto Meschino of Knightsville, an original turn-of-the century arrival freely acknowledged:

> "If I am to be frank, then I shall say that I left Italy and came to America for the sole purpose of finding a better life. I am not influenced by either the government of Italy or the government of America. I suffered no political oppression in Italy, I was not seeking political ideals; as a matter of fact, I was quite satisfied with my native land. If I could have worked my way up in my chosen profession in Italy, I would have stayed there. But repeated efforts showed me that I could not. America was the land of opportunity. I was born in America because my parents came to the United States with the original wave

of immigrants. My mother didn't like it here and was lonely for home so the whole family returned to Itri. When I was seventeen years old I used to hang out in the Piazza with my friends on Saturdays and Sundays,. We all wanted to come to the United States which was truly seen as the land of opportunity. Letters from my relatives in the states, described a life that was much better than we were living. In Itri we were able to eat meat about once a month; in the states there was enough meat to eat every day. My aunt got me a job in construction. Eventually I opened my own landscaping business which was pretty successful and continued to be successful for thirty-five years. I am very proud of my three sons who are all college educated. One is a physician working on an Aids study in Virginia, another is a psychiatrist in California, and the other is a pilot living in England. In some ways I lament providing college education for the boys since they ultimately left Rhode Island for job opportunities elsewhere. I would have liked to have them closer to home." (Personal interview, July 1996)

Depressed by a psychology of scarcity, there is little wonder that whole villages became depopulated. There was little incentive to stay. Italy's inability to mechanize, antiquated methods of cultivation, weak economic growth, land problems, and an uncreative leadership, intensified the appeal of the outside world. The alternative was a life of resignation and patience which had sustained their ancestors for centuries.

THE NEW WORLD

The massive flow of Italian immigrants to the United States after the 1840s has been documented as one of the most extraordinary phenomenon of modern history. Before 1860, the immigration appears to have been of persons who desired permanent settlement. That could be readily explained, without going further, by the difficulties of transportation. Some Italian craftsmen crossed the Atlantic in the seventeenth century. Many were invited such as the Italian glassblowers who settled in Jamestown. In the early records of the English colonies, there are mention of Italian musicians, figure carvers, language teachers, wine merchants and visitors. Italian sculptors, such as Giuseppe Ceracchi, traveled and worked in the new nation during the 1790's. Ceracchi executed portrait busts of

George Washington and John Adams, and while in Philadelphia, tutored American sculptor William Rush. Other Italian sculptors who came to America were Giovanni Andrei and Giuseppe Franzoni. They came at the invitation of Thomas Jefferson to work on the Capitol. Earlier, Jefferson had employed Italian marble cutters to build the University of Virginia and was responsible for recruiting fourteen Italian musicians to form the first marine band.

Italian opera, opera houses built especially for Italian opera, and Italian singers became part of the early cultural life of urban America. Giovanni Grassi, and Italian Jesuit, became president of Georgetown University, Giovanni Nobili and Michael Accolti established Santa Clara College in California, Joseph Cataldo, after an active life spent in Montana, Idaho, Wyoming, Oregon, Alaska and Washington (1867-1928) founded Gonzaga University in Spokane, Washington.

Between 1820 and 1865 approximately 17,000 Italians entered North America settling mainly along the East Coast. In Philadelphia, there were approximately two hundred Italians by 1850; the group grew to three hundred by 1870. In 1880, forty-four hundred Italians lived in the United States. In 1850, there were two hundred Italians living in San Francisco. By 1851, six-hundred Italians had settled in San Francisco. Large scale emigration from Italy began in early nineteenth century from the North. Immigrants traveled from Northern Italy, and they included besides traders, many Lucchese vendors of plaster statuary and street musicians.

The turning point in the history of Italian immigration to the United States was 1880. Every year thereafter, one would find thousands of Italians pouring off the immigrant ships. Described as the era of mass migration, it has been estimated that no fewer than 26 million Italians emigrated between 1861 and 1970, and that since 1900 more than 10 million Italians have left their country permanently. In _The Children of Columbus_, Erik Amfitheatrof states;

> "The exodus of southern Italians from their villages at the turn of the twentieth century has no parallel in history. Out of a total population of fourteen million in the South at the time of national unification in 1860-70, at least five million-over a third of the population-had left to seek work overseas. The

magnitude of this emigration particularly to the United States; is indicated in some of the annual statistics. Between 1900 and 1910, over two million Italians arrived in the United States; in 1907, a total of 285,000 entered; on the eve of World War I in 1914, 296,414 made their way through American ports."

Two forces were at play during the last years of the 19th century and the first decades of the 20th. At the same time, the United States underwent a remarkable change. During this period now known as the Industrial Revolution, new sources of power were developed. Beginning in mid-eighteenth-century England it soon spread to the United States, bringing mechanization. The addition of external sources of power such as the invention of the dynamo in 1867 made the use of electricity practical. Further, the development of the internal combustion in the 1880's revolutionized transportation. These new forms of energy soon rendered cottage industries obsolete. Factories which had become central-ized workplaces apart from the home-rapidly transformed the economy. Whole new industries and mass production changed individual work-manship into machine-made, factory produced products changing the character of work.

As late as 1890, the United States was primarily an agricultural country, with 42 percent of its labor force engaged in farming. Increasing in the last years of the nineteenth and into the twentieth century pros-pects of financial gains in the U.S. existed not in agriculture, but in the large urban centers of the East. Italian immigrants poured in as the need of this country was for increased mill workers and unskilled laborers. At the close of the century following the precedence of Europe, the focus of the American economy began to shift to industry. New factories and mills springing up in every city required a never ending supply of manpower. People migrated from remote villages to towns and cities for factory jobs. The Italians, along with other new immigrant groups provided the labor to run the machinery.

Eighty percent of the Italians who came to the United States were from the Mezzogiorno, the provinces south of Rome. They were peasants (contidini). For the vast majority, emigration offered the best, perhaps the only, hope for improving their lives. By the nineteenth-century Italy was a poverty-stricken land whose only major natural resource was people. These were the agricultural areas of Italy, and at the same time, the poorest. The south of Italy has always been poorer than the north. Centuries of continuous farming had exhausted the soil, and the majority of the peasants lived in a state of never ending poverty.

The peak of Italian immigration was not reached until well into the 20th century. In one year alone Italy sent over 300,000 immigrants—more than the whole population of the city of Venice. From the mid-1880s to the mid-1920s over five million migrated to the United States. In terms of total migration the Italians ranked third behind immigrants from British Isles and Germany.

The first two decades of the 20th century were the great years of Italian immigration. Although the number had been increasing steadily since the 1880's, the pace of immigration quickened after the turn of the century. Between the years of 1901-10 over two million Italians entered the country; from 1911-20, another two million arrived.

Coming to the United States usually involved a complete change in the immigrant's way of life. Newcomers had once been able to find cheap or even free land to farm in our western territories. By the end of the 19th century, when the Italians began to come in significant numbers the frontier was gone and the free land virtually all taken up.

After the initial stage of settlement of any immigrant nationality at its chosen destination, some scattering, however gradual, invariably ensues. Thus one expects subsequent census to show less geographical concentration. As the Italian immigration increased in volume, however, the predominance of the southern element became greater and its concentration became actually more marked. In 1850, just half of the Italian population was within the area included in the census of 1790; but in 1900 three quarters were. In the state of New York there were as many Italians as the entire United States had contained, ten years earlier. Two out of five of all newcomers have gone to large urban areas. Of those in the state in 1910, nearly two-thirds dwelt in its metropolis, 340,770—a number which would probably make an entire large city in Italy; and if their children were added the colony would exceed in population every Italian city, except possibly Naples. The following census chart shows the impact of increasing emigration.

Table 1. Italian Immigration to the United States 1820-1920

1820-1830 439

1831-40 .... 2, 253

1841-50 .... 1, 870

1851-60 9,231

1861-70 .... 11, 725

1871-80 .... 55, 759

1881-90 307,309

1891-1900 651,893

1901-10 2,045,877

1911-20 .... 1,109.524

Based on United States Bureau of the Census, _Historical Statistics of the United States; Colonial Times to 1970_, Part 1, pp. 105-6.

Before World War I, the ratio by gender of Italian immigrants entering the United States was about eighty men to every twenty women. Because of the unknown conditions in the new country and the lack of money with which to make the trip, emigration long remained pre-dominantly a single male activity. After the war, a growing familiarity of the new land coupled with basic human emotional needs gave a new impulse to female immigration. Thereafter whole families increasingly migrated together.

THE TRIP

Most of the newcomers to the new world landed in New York City. The steamship crossing was not a pleasant experience. Most of the peasants had never strayed far from their village, and here they were in the crowded ports of Genoa, Naples and Palermo awaiting departure. On the ships, the quarters were overcrowded and poorly ventilated, and there was limited access to deck space. During bad weather, there were frequent occurrences on the turbulent Atlantic. The women, young children and babies were placed in one compartment and the vastly larger numbers of men and older boys slept in the other compartments. Beds were double or triple-tiered with iron frameworks which supported burlap-covered bags of straw, grass, or waste which served as mattresses. As with most ships which depended on the emigrant trade, little thought was devoted to the comfort of passengers in steerage. There were few diversions on board. Even on sunny days, when they all crowded onto the small deck time passed slowly. Italians tried to come to the aid of each other during the hard voyage. They brought supplies of cheese and salami which supplemented the meager rations doled out by the steamship. Lice, scurvy and seasickness added to their misery. Men and women suffered together the humiliation of public fumigation.

After a steamship crossing that lasted 14 days in 1867, the immigrant's first depot was Castle Garden. It had been an amusement place until it was taken over by the State of New York in 1855. At this reception center, through which everyone had to pass, they were counted, and their ages, occupations, religions, and the value of property they brought with them were recorded. Each immigrant wore a name tag with a letter and number. The immigrants were given physical exams to detect glaucoma and communicable diseases. As each immigrant paused in front of a double row of doctors, they were evaluated. On the coats of about two out of every ten immigrants who passed by the doctor, he would scrawl a large while letter indicating potential diseases; "H" for possible heart trouble; "L" for lameness; "G" for goiter; "Pg" for Pregnancy; "S" for senility; a circled "X" for suspected mental defects, or "F" for a bad rash on the face.

They then had to file past a second doctor who was looking for diseases specifically mentioned in deportation papers; tuberculosis, leprosy, or other contagious diseases. At the next evaluation two doctors with basins of disinfectants and towels, checked the upper eyelids for trachoma. Those who were thought to have the disease had their coats chalked with an "E" for eyes.

Those whose coats bore chalk letters were pushed into a pen for a more detailed medial exam. Those whose coats were unmarked could proceed to the section where they were queried about their past and future; "What work do you do?' – 'Do you have a job waiting here for you?" – 'Who paid for your passage?" –'Is anyone meeting you?' – 'Where are you going?' – 'How much money do you have?' – 'Where did you get it?' If the immigrant successfully passed this questioning they could purchase items like bread, milk, and coffee and use the extensive kitchen facilities to prepare their own food. Once through Castle Garden foreigners dispersed quickly. Those without the financial means to travel stayed in New York. In 1892, according to United States Bureau of Immigration statistics, Italian immigrants brought into the country an average of only $11.00 per person. Others, determined to reach their destination quickly purchased railroad tickets or were met by relatives to assist them.

In 1892, Ellis Island became the main clearing house for immigrants under the aegis of the federal government. Twenty-five million passed through its gates between its inception and the time it was closed in 1954. The year that brought the greatest influx was 1907, when a daily average of five thousand aliens crowded Ellis Island, straining the capacity of the depot and the patience of immigration officials. Ellis Island closed in 1954, and was reopened in 1976 as a tourist attraction. It is now a national shrine. Not far from Ellis Island stands a symbol of freedom and hope, The Statue of Liberty. A gift of the French people in 1885, in commemoration of the hundredth anniversary of American independence, it became a symbol of welcome to millions of newcomers. Many wept at the sight of her and at the same time experienced an affirmation of the hopes and dreams that had caused them to leave home, family, and friends in order to follow a distant dream.

EARLY LIFE IN THE UNITED STATES

An estimated 97 percent of Italians coming to the United States landed in New York City. By 1903, there were 1.2 million Italians in the United States. About twelve percent of that number lived in New York City. New York City's population grew from 1 million in 1895 to 3.5 million in 1900. From there some fanned out through the country although they remained close to the port of arrival or settled in urban-industrial centers. Life in the Italian communities in America during the period of the great migrations was indescribably difficult. Necessity, ignorance of the dangers involved, and the lack of resources led the newly arrived Italian immigrants into the slums of the poorest sections of cities and into rundown houses. The cities of the nineteenth century were unprepared for the heavy influx of population which was caused by increasing immigration as well as by the movement of once rural inhabitants to the cities. The consequence was that once beautiful cities had increasingly become defaced by slums. The journalist reformer Jacob Riis provided a vivid description of 1890 life in the Mulberry Street slum in lower Manhattan which housed a great congregation of Italians:

> "The Italians sought out the cheapest, the oldest and worst tenements. Where ever they went, the houses sank to the Italian level. They were content with a pigsty and let the rent collector rob them. In the Mulberry Street Bend were the most squalid tenements; once cow bells tinkled there, but now the bells announced the home-coming, rag-pickers carts. In a single block, there had been 155 deaths of children under five. The Italians vice was his dirtiness; he was dirtier than the Negro and the Bend was scarce dirtier than the Little Italy of Harlem. Most tenements hold ten to thirty families. A whole family, of eight or ten men, may sleep in a room. On hot nights, every fire escape becomes a bedstead."

The concentration of Italians in the slum areas of large cities and in low-paying occupations was a source of deep concern to contemporary observers. Erik Amfitheatrof adds the following grim observations concerning this problem:

> "In one block in Mulberry Street, in 1888, the death rate for both adults and children was high. In perpetually dark, airless rear tenements as many as a third of all babies died before their first birthday."

Jacob Riis wrote on this topic also:

> "In summer, despite the efforts of special teams of doctors and nurses, the gravediggers in Calvary work over-time, and little coffins are stacked mountains high on the deck of the Charity Commissioners boat when it makes its semi-weekly trips to the city cemetery."

But the Italian peasant survived in this sort of purgatory, if not in the Bend then in similar slums in other large urban settings.

WORK AND THE PADRONE

The search for employment was a major factor determining where Italians would settle. If he were fortunate to have a relative or paisano (townsman or fellow villager) on hand to meet him, and provide a job the problem was solved. Italians as helpless newcomers have had to accept low wages, less than a living wage according to American standards. Only a fraction of the newcomers could continue their traditional occupations. The majority had to find work as they could. Most could not speak the language of their new home. Many had only a hazy idea of what life was like in America. The immigrants were most often brought over by labor contractors. Agents of steamship companies and labor contractors covered the countryside of Italy in their search for workers. In their recruiting efforts they depicted the United States as a land of plenty, where taxes were negligible, liberty assured, and food and work plentiful. Frequently the contractors were Italians, called padrones, who had lived for a few years in the New World and discovered the manpower needs of American Industry. They would return to their native villages and enlist others offering enticements intended to recruit services for their boss. By advancing passage money, the contractors would bring in whole shiploads of potential laborers.

The Italian padrones exercised great control over immigrant's lives. The padrones, who had come to the United States earlier, spoke English and arranged jobs and found living accommodations for their later-arriving compatriots. The immigrant worker did not have to be afraid to travel in a foreign land or remain out of work for lack of money. The padrone would make sure he was escorted to the work site and maintain a close vigilance over him until the job was completed. Men and boys were sent off to railroad and constructions gangs, lumber camps, and factories. A padrone collected the salaries of everyone under him, or else a prior fee for placement, and kept a portion for himself as his commission. He also performed sundry tasks like writing letters and sending money back home for those unable to do so themselves. Often, and accurately, accused of taking advantage of those who placed their trust in him, the record of abuses committed by the padrone is replete with reports of decrepit rooming houses and vanishing payrolls. The padrone nonetheless performed the valuable services of easing the adjustment to the New World and of obtaining a man's initial position for him. In 1897, two thirds of the Italian workers in New York were controlled by padrone, but as the immigrant numbers increased and the states began to regulate labor agents, the need for this intermediary lessened.

The padrone system was a widespread institution among the immigrants. The early fortunes of Italian immigrants in America are bound up with this unique social institution. An intermediary was needed to negotiate between the large numbers of Italian laborers, helpless as to language and knowledge of labor opportunities, and American employers, who were equally helpless in recruiting workers.

The labor force that was employed for the industrial expansion of the United States at the turn of the century was drawn in large part from southern Europe. Most of the wage earners engaged in manufacturing and mining at the time were foreign born. These immigrants worked in the iron and copper mines of the Mid-West, Southwest and South. They were found in the steel plants and glass factories of the Middle West and South. They worked in the mines, mills, and factories of the east and traveled throughout the country providing the labor for temporary and seasonal needs. In the west and mid-west they did construction work or harvest work from spring to fall. In winter they kept busy at logging camps or brought in ice off of the Great Lakes. In the south most Italians worked on the railroads, carrying cross-ties, shifting tracks, and doing pick and shovel tasks. Others served as general laborers, cotton pickers and sugar cane cutters. In terms of rural labor, from May to October they would go berry picking as the crops matured; strawberries, blackberries, raspberries and cranberries. According to one source, during those years farmers would contract with padrones in early spring to ensure enough harvesters. The padrone would canvass the neighborhoods and induce immigrants to sign up with them, promising free shelter, straw with which to fill their bed tickings, inexpensive fruit and vegetables, and a net profit for the season from $150 to $400. The padrone would get a salary of $1.50 to $3.00 a day from the farmer. But they received their greatest commission by providing the usual commissary, transportation and banking services to their workers.

THE ARRIVAL OF FAMILIES

In the early years of the mass exodus from southern Italy, it was usually the men who left, returned, and then emigrated once again. Known as "Sojourners" or "economic opportunists" they came simply to make money and then return to Italy to buy land and settle down. In later years, they began to think of America as a new and permanent home. The man who had left his family behind saved his earnings for their passage so that wives and children could now join him. The immigrants made homes for themselves in America. They would ultimately learn that the belief that the streets were paved with gold was, of course, a far cry from reality.

For the women, leaving Italy was difficult. If married, women wanted to join their husbands. But the unmarried woman was overcome with romantic sentiment, often based on myth. Early settlers in America had sent letters vividly describing the bountiful conditions with glowing accounts of life. Many of these messages conveyed the unwarranted impression that quick fortunes could be made here. In many instances, these letters exaggerated reality so that immigrants could save face to those left behind. These exaggerations came to be enmeshed in the powerful attraction of the new world. Two reminiscences from literature offered romantic impressions of Italian life in America. The "Southern Literary Messenger" of December 1842 printed the anonymous "letters of an Italian Exile." C. Giardini's "Gli Stati Uniti" (Bologna, 1887) relates how 300 Italian miners joyfully walked five miles laden with gifts and fruit, which they laid at the feet of the first Italian woman to grace the state of California. That image must have certainly been an extremely powerful motivating factor for the Itrani woman.

My own mother an Itrani woman, Maria Civita Fabrizio related the impact these letters had on her decision to come to America:

> "I was twenty-one and still single, helping my family. An older woman nearby my home, had received some letters from a man she knew who had been born in Itri and left for America. He expressed a desire to find a nice Italian wife, preferably from Itri. Did she know of someone for him, he wrote? She told me about the letters which described America as a great country, large and beautiful, with so much money that the streets were paved with gold. It sounded like a paradise. After all, what did I have in Itri and what could I look forward to? This woman advised me to marry this man so that I could go to America and live like a Queen". (Personal interview)

The community of Itrani was so tight that most of the immigrant men from Itri made sure that they married women from Itri. This was usually arranged by neighbors and friends through the mail as was the case with my own parents.

The women who emigrated with their families or to join husbands also found employment. Depending on the location and the availability of work, Italian women contributed to the family income. In Buffalo, New York, women worked in the canneries outside the city; throughout the truck-farming areas across America they helped harvest crops; in Providence, Rhode Island, they worked in factories or at home making jewelry; in Chicago, women shelled and sorted nuts, made candy, and worked in the men's clothing industry; in New York City women made artificial flowers and children's toys and finished clothing at home or in factory lofts; and in Tampa, Florida Italian women worked in the cigar industry.

Children also were part of the economic enterprise. In Italy, compulsory education, when established and enforced, provided three years of rudimentary instruction. Many immigrants were semi-literate. The rate of illiteracy for women was even higher, since education was considered an unnecessary luxury for most. In America, much of this traditional attitude continued. Most children left school as early as the law allowed so that they could begin to work. Parents were caught between the lure of free education and the economic necessities of life.

Despite the departure of less-successful workers during depression years Italian immi-

WEDDING PHOTO OF MARIA CIVITA FABRIZIO AND GIACINTO DELUCA IN ITRI-1920

FAMILY WEDDING PHOTO—ITRI-1920

gration after the turn of the century became more stable as women and children joined the men who came seeking their fortunes. As early as 1901, it was recognized that after a few years either the family was brought over or, if the man was single, he married and settled down here, becoming a permanent member of the community.

• •

The exodus of the contidini from southern Italy was prompted by many factors including; social disruption caused by the struggle for the unification of Italy; a dramatic population increase in southern Italy during the later 19th century; the depressed state of Italian agriculture including the exploitation of the contidini by absentee landlords; the excessive subdivision (frazionamento) of all land following the abolition of the primogeniture and the heavy incidence of malaria. The contadinis' desire for economic improvement prompted their migration to the new world. Recruitment campaigns were conducted in southern Italy by American industrialists and steamship lines. Coupled with the reduction of steamship fares to the United States by 30 percent between the years of 1896-1904, these factors facilitated the Italian exodus.

L'EMIGRANTE

Di Francesco A. Canella, Cranston, Rhode Island
(Reprinted with permission.)

La Casa sua lascia L'emigrante
Sa che lascia I suoi cari tutti quanti;
Lascia coloro che l'han visto crescere;
Partendo si raccomanda alla Madonna e ai santi.

Quanto giunge alla terra destinata
La nostalgia gli piglia di cio' che ha lasciato
E pensa...forse il venire qui e' stata un' ide sbagliata
Ma dopo un poco anche questa crisi ha superato.

Nuove idée incomminciano a venire
Prima una bella automobile si vuol compare
Poi una bella casa. Che c'e' da dire?
Quanto si lavora, tutto si puo' fare

Poi ci ripensa...sarebbe meglio guadagnare tantisoldi
E dopo pochi anni al mio paese ritonare;
Di tanto in tanto ritornano I vecchi ricordi
E su tanti progetti si mette a fantasticare.

Ma piano piano il tempo passa
E di tornare al suo paese non piu' gli piace;
Si vede piu' libero, e in mezzo a tanta grassa
E di restare si rassegna in santa pace.

E con questa non commune rassaegnazione
Da millenni mai si ferma l'emigrante;
Un grande aiuto da' alla sua nuova nazione
Facendo ogni cosa piccolo diventar grande.

THE IMMIGRANT

By Francesco A. Canella, Cranston, Rhode Island

The immigrant leaves his village home,
Hoping to find his fortune in other lands.
So many splendid dreams fill his heart
Yet, one by one tears trickle down his face.

He knows he leaves the village of his birth,
He knows he leaves all his dear ones behind.
He leaves all those who watched him growing up.
Taking leave he entrusts himself,
To the Madonna and Saints.

Upon arriving in the destined land,
He is overcome by longing for that left behind.
And he thinks, maybe I was wrong to come here.
But after awhile this crisis too, he overcomes.

He begins to discover new dreams.
First he thinks to buy a new car.
Then a nice home, and why not?
When there is work, everything is possible.

Then he has second thoughts;
Perhaps it's better to earn a lot of money,
And after a few years return to my native town.
From time to time all the old memories return.

But little by little the years pass by.
The dream of returning home loses its appeal
He sees himself freer in the midst of plenty.
He resigns himself to stay and be content.

And thus coming to terms with his new life;
The immigrant moves ever forward.
He does treat service to his new country;
Making every little thing become great.

CHAPTER 2

CRANSTON: THE MOST ITALIAN OF ALL AMERICAN CITIES

Facts on Italian-American Settlements in the United States:
- Some 12.2 million of U.S. residents are of Italian parentage.
- Most Italian immigrants originally settle in New Jersey, New York, and Pennsylvania; these three states have the greatest Italian-American population.
- Most Italian-Americans live in the Northeast. The rest are equally divided among the Middle West, South, and West.
- Italians make up over 16% of Rhode Island population, the largest portion.
- Cranston, Rhode Island has the greatest proportion of Italian-Americans totaling 38%. Proportions of 25% or more are found in Waterbury, Connecticut; Yonkers, New York; and Providence, Rhode Island.

From the beginning of their immigration Italians settled primarily in large urban communities. These ethnic communities have tended to be along the Eastern Seaboard, particularly New York City and the cities of Rhode Island, Connecticut, Massachusetts, and New Jersey. The trend has continued to this century. The 1960 census shows that about 70 percent of first and second generation Italians was concentrated in the north-eastern portion of America.

In 1980 more than one-half of all persons of Italian ancestry lived in the Northeast. Fewer than 29 percent of all Italians lived in each of the other regions—North Central, South and West.

REGION	NUMBER	PERCENT
Total, U.S.	12,183,692.	100
Northeast	6,929,876.	57
North Central	1,995,424.	16
South	1,555,340.	13
West	1,703,052.	14

Also in the 2000 U.S. Census, in terms of proportions of Italians by state, the highest are: Rhode Island (20.1%), Connecticut (20%), New Jersey (18.4%), and New York (14.8%). Of the twenty-three U.S. cities with the highest proportions of Italians, Cranston, Rhode Island had the highest-38% of the city's population was Italian.

IMMIGRATION TO RHODE ISLAND

It was in April 1524 that Giovanni da Verrazzano, a mariner from Florence, Italy set foot in what is now Rhode Island. For fifteen days, Verrazzano explored the entire region of Narragansett Bay. Commissioned to find a westward passage to the Orient by Francis I, King of France, Verrazzano explored the northeast coast of North America. In his July 8TH, report to the King, Verrazzano described his springtime visit to the Narragansett region. He had arrived first at Block Island, where he noted the many tree-covered hills; it seemed to him to be about the size of the Island of Rhodes, an observation that later gave Rhode Island its name. His meticulous description of the islands in Narragansett Bay and of its inhabitants was the first written records of Rhode Island by a European explorer.

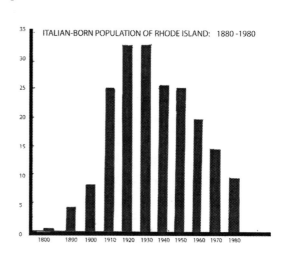

ITALIAN BORN POPULATION OF RHODE ISLAND: 1880-1980

Very few Italians were to follow Verrazzano to Rhode Island for the next three hundred years. Prior to 1850, information was not collected regarding nativity, so there are no certain numbers before that date. However, by the 1850 census, records indicate that there were 25

Italian-born residents in the state. The federal census of 1880 showed only 313 Italians out of a total population of 276,531 in Rhode Island. As of 1890 this figure had grown to about 2,500.

The first known Italian to settle in Rhode Island was Joseph Carlo Mauran (Giuseppe Carlo Maurani), founder of the distinguished Mauran family in Rhode Island. A pioneer in a new country is always an interesting person, and Joseph Mauran who came during the early colonial period was certainly one. Italy as an emigratory country was one of the last great nations to send its sons to the U.S. Some of the earliest Italians were seamen. Giuseppe, a native of Villafranca, near Nice, Italy was one of them. Born on June 3, 1748, Giuseppe was 12 years old and was sailing with a relative in the Mediterranean Sea in a small vessel, bound for Sardinia. The vessel was overtaken by a British man-of-war, and the two boys were impressed into the British service as cabin boys. The other boy, whose name was Sucket, died of small pox. After two years of captivity the ship on which Mauran was cabin boy came into New London Harbor. Young Mauran was in the bow of the boat and as the boat touched the land, he sprang out and ran to a field where some farmers drove the sailors away. They helped him to make good his escape. He came to Westerly, Rhode Island, where he found a home in the family of Daniel Maxon.

Leaving Westerly in 1768, Mauran went to Barrington and entered the employ of Joshua Bicknell, a farmer. In 1772, Mauran married Mr. Bicknell's daughter Olive. She received at her marriage a parcel of land on the Barrington River, just south of the old White Church, and there the Maurans made their home and made their home.

Mauran served with distinction in the war for American independence. In 1775, the Rhode Island General Assembly ordered the construction of two "row galleys" or gunboats, the "Washington" and the "Spitfire", each to carry sixty men. In March 1776, Mauran then only 28 years of age, was placed in command of the Spitfire, which had several engagements with the British. In April 1776, the two vessels were sent to New York to be placed under the orders of General Washington. The original Washington was "blown up" in April 1777, but was soon repaired and rigged as a schooner. Captain Mauran was placed in command of her. In May 1778, a body of British and Hessian troops attached Warren and burned a number of boats, including the Washington which was undergoing repairs in the Kickemuit River, east of town. The British then went to Bristol and burned a number of houses but 0before they could destroy the entire village, they were attacked by an armed force of Americans and driven back to their landing place. It is said that Captain Mauran played an important part in this engagement by bringing up a cannon, which did heavy damage to the invaders. Later in the war Captain Mauran was in command of the privateer schooner Weazle, bearing letters of marque and reprisal from the Governor of Rhode Island.

After serving in the war, Captain Mauran was the master of various vessels in ocean commerce. He retired from his sea-faring life and spent his later years in Barrington, where he died in his 65th year on May 1, 1813.

During the early colonial period, the earliest Italians were seamen from Genoa, wandering harp players, vendors of plaster statues, farmers, groups of street organ players, and special artists. The early Italians who came to the U.S. up to the 1870's were a few isolated groups. It wasn't until the 1880's that Italians take their place as a migratory people. From the 1880's until 1914, it contributed in augmenting the population of Rhode Island. In the Sunday, October 7, 1888 edition of the Providence Journal, a column addressed this increase in presence of Italians in Providence as well as the contributions and progress they are making. It noted:

> Within the past two years the Italian population has increased by over 500 persons. Most of the emigrants are from the south of the Italian peninsula, more properly termed the Neapolitan provinces. The foundation of the Italian colony in Providence dates from 1832, one of the earliest to arrive was the later George M. Ardonene, who by dint of hard work and close attention to business became the leading caterer of this city. Mr. Ardoene was largely instrumental in obtaining many advantages for his fellows, and, in fact, for many years was the only person who they could look to for assistance. Those were the halcyon days of the peanut vendor and organ grinder, a race now almost extinct in Providence. On almost every corner on Westminster, Broad, Weybosset, and North Main streets were graced by the Italian with his fruit and candy stand. It is a mystery to many how all these Italians live, and there is a prevailing

opinion among many others that organ grinding, peanut selling chestnut roasting, and a few such other occupations is all that the average Italian does or is fit for. This, however, is a great mistake, for today there are about five Italian fruit stands in Providence located on the southerly side of Exchange place, and there is just one resident organ grinder, and he in his peculiar vernacular says; "Me dia di hunga, nota maka one penna." It is in the large manufacturing establishments that the Italians must be looked for today, and it is to their credit that they prefer steady work in the mill or at out door labor rather than to somewhat vagabond life of the itinerant musician or fruit vendor. The musician is still here, but his chords and rhapsodies are confined to private yards by day, and the more remote beer saloons at night. Occasionally he appears in the costume of his mountain home, but so grimy and dilapidated that none of the poetry invoked by the picturesque peasants depicted in novels and on stage, is possible when he is seen wearily trudging up Atwell's Avenue, hugging his equally dilapidated violin under his coat. But even the musician is fast disappearing, and no less than three of them who have accumulated a few dollars have within the past three months opened small groceries in the haunts of their compatriots.

Large scale Italian immigration to Rhode Island took place between 1900 and 1915. By 1900, there were nearly 9,000 Italian foreign-born living in the state. By 1910, that figure tripled to 27,000 Italians. By 1920, one Rhode Islander out of every nine was of Italian extraction. This increase was also due to the fact that from 1911, to the outbreak of World War I, Providence became one of nation's major immigrant-landing stations after the Fabre Steamship Line located there. The Italian strength in numbers for the most part went unnoticed until the Columbus Day celebration in Providence that year. In Rhode Island: Three Centuries of Democracy, historian Charles Carroll recorded the event:

"For hours, Italian divisions poured through the city streets in rapid succession at steady military pace, unceasingly and apparently inexhaustively.....Rhode Island had become conscious of its Italian population in a day"

In that year, the Italian-Americans were recorded as the largest number of foreign-born of any ethnic group in the state.

Rhode Island on the eve of the twentieth century offered an ideal center for the Italian. Few other states were better suited to absorb the invasion of a traditionally industrious population. The cities of Rhode Island were alive with the sounds of construction. Major municipal buildings projects, such as the State House constructed between 1896, and 1901, and a streetcar tunnel completed by 1914, provided immigrants with jobs as unskilled construction workers, excavators, and hod carriers. Other unskilled laborers and former agricultural workers found work in the jewelry shops, foundries, machine shops and textile mills that filled the cities. While many Italian immigrants were familiar with the pick and shovel-tools of the laborer-the factories were new workplaces. Italian laborers looked for work with stable conditions and familiar faces. Many gravitated to the more secure jobs, working for the city or for the railroad, jobs that they kept for thirty and forty years. All of these early industries were overshadowed in the early nineteenth century by the coming of the textile industry. Based on the factory system, the American textile industry—which was born in Rhode Island sparked the beginnings of the American Industrial Revolution. Rhode Island became the nations' most industrialized state. The nineteenth century saw the real establishment of the four big Rhode Island industries; textiles, metal trades, jewelry and silver-smiths, and rubber. By 1831 Rhode Island boasted 116 cotton mills. By the Civil War the number had jumped to 153. Closely following cotton was woolen manufacturers. The establishment of textile industries led to a demand for iron and steel for machinery and building. Foundries, machine shops, screw and nail factories, gun shops— factories of all kinds became established. The outstanding silver craftsmanship of Rhode Island led naturally to commercial silver production, laying the foundation for the present Gorham Company. Nehemiah Dodge became founder of what has become the large costume jewelry industry in Rhode Island when he developed a process of plating gold on copper in 1800.

To run its industrial system, Rhode Island needed cheap labor. The state became a lodestone for immigrants from Europe. Although the Irish predominated, the French Canadians were rapidly catching up. Then after 1890, a tremendous influx of Italians raised the total number of Italians to 27,000 by 1910.

The great majority of these newcomers to Rhode Island were of the peasant class. They followed the same patterns of migration as elsewhere in the United States. During a thirty-four year period a total of 54,973 Italian arrivals landed at the port of Providence. Of that total of 54,973, 3,054 were designated "northerners," while the remaining 51,919 were identified as coming from the south of Italy. As they poured into the port of Providence off of the ships of the Fabre Line, they headed to where their paesani had settled. For example, immigrants from Fornelli chose West Warwick's village of Natick; those from the mountain towns of Aliano, Raviscania, and Saint' Angelo D'Alife settled in West Barrington. From Calabria, Cocenza, and Acri, the new arrivals went to Westerly; from Itri they made Cranston's village of Knightsville their new home.

CRANSTON

Cranston was probably settled in 1638 by some of the Providence associates of Roger Williams. Three of the prominent early settlers were William Harris, Zachariah Rhodes, and William Arnold. The latter was the father of Benedict Arnold. Harris was the political leader of

ITALIAN IMMIGRANTS DEBARKING FROM THE FABRE STEAMSIP LINE'S SHIP, VENEZIA IN PROVIDENCE-1913—PHOTO COURTESY OF RHODE ISLAND HITORICAL SOCIETY

the early residents; he carried on a long dispute with Roger Williams, claiming that Providence had no jurisdiction over the present Cranston. In 1754, the Pawtuxet River and adjacent settlements were incorporated as the township of Cranston, in honor of Samuel Cranston of Newport, Governor of the Colony 1698-1727. It was incorporated as a city in 1910.

There were 1,460 inhabitants in Cranston at the time of its incorporation. In the census of Rhode Island in the year 1885, there were 8 males and 2 females for a total of 10 residents whose place of birth was listed as Italy. By the year 1895, there were 97 males and 50 females for a total of 147 residents whose birthplace was listed as Italy. By 1921, the Italian population numbered approximately 3,500 which was more than any other ethnic group residing in the city.

Cranston is described as a city of contrasts, heavily populated in the east and largely rural in the west. It does not have an urban character. The city consists of approximately thirty square miles stretching from Narragansett Bay on the east to the town of Scituate in the west. Routes I-95 and I-295 run north-south through the city, providing direct access to Providence and other major east-coast cities. Geography has played an important role in shaping the city's history. With good topsoil throughout, Cranston was predominantly an agricultural community for two-and-a-half centuries. Gristmills and sawmills dotted the countryside. In addition, minor deposits of iron ore, coal, gravel, and granite all exist beneath the surface of the land and each has been mined or quarried over the years. The advent of the automobile and post-World War I highway construction combined to transform central Cranston from a broad green swatch of truck farms into a classic mid-twentieth-century suburb. Numerous one-story ranch houses are set back from winding roads of subdivisions.

Although an agricultural city, Cranston became the site of important mills. In 1820 there were already seven cotton factories and three woolen-goods mills in operation. The rise of Cranston as an industrial center dates from the early 19th century when the textile factory, now known as the Cranston Print Works, was opened. The Print Works, which was the city's first important industrial enterprise was located in Knightsville and would prove to be a major attraction for emigrants to Rhode Island. Most of the early Italian immigrants worked in the booming textile industry. Smaller percentages engaged in agriculture and domestic service.

KNIGHTSVILLE

The principal village of the town of Cranston is Knightsville, set at the approximate center of Cranston. Knightsville began to emerge as the town's civic center shortly after the turn of the 19th century. The use of Nehemiah Knight's tavern for town meetings and the importance of his family's role in town and state government make Knightsville a natural political center. Knight served as town clerk from 1773 to 1800 and as U.S. Congressman from 1803 to 1808. His son Nehemiah

R.Knight was governor of Rhode Island (1817-1821) and served in the U.S. Senate from 1821-1841. Jeremiah Knight, Jr. succeeded his uncle serving as town clerk from 1803-1821. Cranston's first bank was established in the Knightsville home of Jeremiah Knight in 1818. Though somewhat altered, the two-and-half story, central-chimney building remains at 275 Phenix Avenue. Throughout the first half of the nineteenth century, Knightsville continued to grow, due both to its role as civic center and its proximity to emerging industrial centers.

MAP OF KNIGHTSVILLE, RHODE ISLAND

WORK FOR THE IMMIGRANTS

In Knightsville, natural water power sites, deposits of iron ore, coal, gravel and granite, and the Cranston Print Works, the agricultural businesses of James Budlong and John M. Dean initially attracted settlers to the area. The Cranston Print Works was originated by William Sprague in 1807 when he converted a small grist mill into one of the first cotton mills in New England. Although farming was the Sprague families' only interest, the invention of the machinery for spinning cotton in 1808 changed the direction of their interest. The A & W Sprague Company was one of their first companies and was located on the present site of the Cranston Print Works. Through the years Sprague enterprises sprung up everywhere and ultimately consisted of nine mills, controlling interest in many industries, and three banks. The Sprague family produced two Rhode Island State Assemblymen and two Governors who went on to become U.S. Senators. The family was nationally prominent in the 1860s. William Sprauge III's wedding to the daughter of the Chief Justice of the U.S. Supreme Court was attended by President Lincoln and his entire cabinet.

Cranston's effort to rise as an industrial center can be traced to the Cranston Print Works which holds the unique distinction of being Cranston's oldest industry. It was the city's first major industrial enterprise. Calico printing in this country was first begun and received much of its early development in this plant. It is still considered to be one of the largest calico printing companies in the world. The Cranston Print Works was the center of a classic mill village or "factory village" effected by the Industrial Revolution in America—where significant activities of an economic, political, and social nature were begun, owned , and controlled by the proprietors of the mill. Print Work Village (Knightsville) became a classic 19th century company town, complete with company store. By 1869 over two thousand workers lived there in company housing. As with most other factory villages throughout the United States, the economic, political and social influences exerted by the Cranston Print Works were substantial. Economically the Print Works were an economic asset to Cranston. Tax records indicate that the firm was the town's largest taxpayer during its growth years, contributing from approximately five per cent to twenty per cent of the total tax income. The firms also made great progress in accumulating real and personal property in the town of Cranston. The year 1868, was the banner year with the firm paying one-fifth of the town's total tax.

Economic power can also lead to social control within the community. The Spragues were responsible for creating a social instrument which has been the most significant contribution to the growth and development of Cranston—the Village. Alternately called Cranston Print Works Village and Sprague's Village or Cranston Village, the village was home to the workers. Since the Print Works owned by the Spragues was the economic life of the village, they controlled industrial relations as well as the religion, education and recreation of the inhabitants of the village.

The Spragues were hard-headed businessmen. Since they were not interested in frills, they laid out their factory villages by careful planning. The cottages, in which the workers resided were built after a uniform model and consisted of seventy-six double cottages and three single-family homes—rows of uniform 1 ½ story gable-roofed structures each with simple Greek revival detailing and painted white. It was the most efficient way to build as dozens of boards were sawed at the same time, saving time and money.

The cottages were neat, comfortable residences, built parallel to the street. Each house was set close to the street allowing a great deal of space in the backyard for tenant use. The double cottages were divided in the middle, having two six-room apartments. The back doors touched each other opening upon a common granite staircase, an arrangement which suggests the promotion of harmony as well as economy. If individuality was desired, the residents could sit apart outdoors on the front steps, which did not adjoin. The rows of unfenced back yards contained two essential items of community life. A well, with windlass and buckets, served every four houses and sometimes as many as eighteen families. The other essential item was an outhouse; one provided for every four houses. Besides the construction of the tenements for those having families, the Spragues built a large three story boarding house for the single worker.

The Company offered prizes for keeping up the property. Regular inspections were made and ruinous practices discouraged. Today, although no longer all white and despite some alterations, the houses of the village, with their uniform setbacks, building heights and massing, constitute a street scene evocative of the classic 19th century mill village.

Cranston established the seat of its government there and Spragueville became the civic center. The Town Clerk's office, and the Police Station was placed close by. With its own water and gas system, steam fire engine company with a hook and ladder and hose car all horse drawn, and great farms for raising sheep and poultry, it became a small city in itself.

A classified advertisement of the period indicates that children were employed at the Print Works. A sample of such an ad follows:

FAMILIES WANTED

10 or 12 good respectable families consisting of 4 or 5 children each, from 9 to 16 years of age, are wanted to work in a Cotton Mill, in the vicinity of Providence. Also, are wanted at the same place, between 15 And 20 steady industrious females, to work upon Water Looms, for information call upon William Sprauge, Jr. at Natick Village—the highest wages will be given to such as can be recommended.

Figures as to the number of children employed are unavailable. However in his biography, Robert Knight, a member of the firm of B.B. & R. Knight which acquired the Cranston Print Works in 1888, left his father's Cranston farm at the age of eight years and took his first job with the Sprague Print Works in 1834. He reports that his workday was sometimes fourteen hours long, and he earned as much as $1.25 a week. Although the Spragues Mills were the "richest in New England" their workers labored for two dollars a week. Good spinners made $2.50 to $3.00 a week, weavers from $3.00 to $5.00 per week, and overseers received $6.00 to $7.00 dollars a week. Young children drew a wage of fifty cents a week. Yet, the Spragues had the reputation of paying as high a wage for labor as any other firm in the state and for paying promptly. Wages were ready on payday and paid in cash.

THE BRICK STORE

The store owned by the Sprauges was said to be a fine, clean, superior store. The goods were of the very best quality and priced competitively. The Spragues did their own slaughtering, and killed about twenty-five head of cattle per week, which were sold to their workers. The store sold every necessary product needed by their workers, if they did not have cash the purchases were made against the wages of the next pay. All family purchases were made at the company store and mostly everything was charged against wages earned. Employees were paid once a month as one of the older employees of the Works said, "We often wound up owing the company."

WORKING HOURS

Most of the population of the Village working at the Print Works had their lives regulated by the factory. Working hours were extremely long. From September to March, the hours were from 5:00a.m. to 8:00p.m. with a half-hour for lunch. The mill bell was the village clock. Advantage was taken of the day light. Candles were used at first, then whale oil lamps followed by kerosene lamps and lanterns. Foot stoves were used for heat. No provision was made to care for the injured.

RELIGIOUS INFLUENCES

There is evidence that the Spragues controlled not only the social conduct but also the religious conduct of their employees. Amasa Sprague I, felt as did most other employers at the time that a man working for him was duty-bound to devote all of his energies to a full, hard day's work at the factory. In addition, he felt that it was his duty to regulate the lives of his employees during their non-working hours as well as during their working hours, even to the extent of their religious practices. The religious welfare of the villagers was attended to by ministers of different denominations employed by the Spragues through contributions. The original place of worship was a church conveniently placed on Cranston Street, across from the Print Works.

POLITICAL INFLUENCES

Knightsville has always been prominent in the politics of Rhode Island. It is the birthplace of six governors, three of whom sat in the Senate of the United States. The first of these governors was Jeremiah R. Knight, a member of the family who owned the land upon which Knight was reared and in whose honor it was named. He served as governor of Rhode Island from 1817-1821. The Sprague family produced two Rhode Island Assemblymen and two Governors who went on to become U.S.Senators. William Sprague was governor during the years 1838-1839, having been elected at the age of 39. William Sprague, the second of this name to be chief executive, was Civil War Governor, 1860-1863, and U.S. Senator, 1863-1875.

Thus, Knightsville as the seat of government continued with this tradition with the Spragues who were prominent in local politics, and had state-wide political power. So great was their political influence, that the Spragues played a role in suppressing the suffrage movement in Cranston. In 1868, the Town of Cranston located the seat of its government in Spragueville in a building owned by the Spragues. The Spragues blatantly used their political influence for economic gains, as well as for personal satisfaction.

Although the Spragues had political and economic influence in the City of Cranston, their most memorable influence has been of a social nature. They created their own community, a factory village which they called Spragueville, and they controlled it according to the dictates of their own conscience. They dictated the rents, wages, food prices, clothing prices, and the working hours, living accommodations and religious practices of their employees.

In 1873, the Sprague failure presented Rhode Island with its severest financial shock. The manufacturing and financial interests of the State and New England were seriously affected. Rhode Island recovered very slowly from this economic blow. The complicated litigation emanating from the Sprague failure flooded the courts of Rhode Island and some of these cases even reached the United States Supreme Court.

In 1888 the Cranston Print Works was acquired by B.B. & R. Knight. The Knights continued the paternalistic pattern of operation set by the Spragues until well into the twentieth century.

These were the conditions that preceded the majority of Italians immigrating to Cranston. Manual labor would be the lot of Cranston's first Italians, whether in the mills or on the local farms. To them would be given the difficult, labor-intensive jobs set aside for the unskilled. Italians played an important part in the textile industries in and around Cranston and the Cranston Print Works, as well are the truck farming industry which was equally demanding. By 1904 the new Italians had constituted the majority of workers in these industries.

TRUCK FARMING THE BUDLONG FARM AND JOHN M. DEAN FARM

Despite increased suburban development in Cranston, most of the town remained largely agricultural into the twentieth century. There were 158 farms in Cranston, producing 262,000 gallons of milk and 36,000 bushels of potatoes a year, including more strawberries, string beans, and green peas that any other town. Throughout the truck-farming areas across America the Italians were harvesting crops. These farms thrived as truck farms with the foremost truck farm in Cranston being the Budlong Farm, begun as a market garden after the Civil War. Budlong first specialized in asparagus, horseradish and pickling cucumbers, but soon included other vegetables which were all trucked to Boston and New York. In 1901, Budlong began raising roses, and by 1937 Budlong Rose Company had 13 acres under glass and produced 18,000 cut roses a day. Its specialty was a double white Killarney. The Budlong Farms workers were originally Swedes, but as of 1937 the employees were largely Italians. As factory jobs in Providence beckoned the Swedes, their jobs were taken in the closing years of the century by the new wave of Italians, immigrating form the village of Itri to the Knightsville section in Cranston.

TURN OF THE CENTURY IMMIGRANT WORKERS AT BUDLONG FARMS IN CRANSTON - PHOTO COURTESY OF CRANSTON HISTORICAL SOCIETY

Although life in their new surroundings was difficult and their reception less than cordial, the Itrani got to work and began a new life. The first Itrani, most of them men, came to Knightsville in the latter year of the 19th century. Their greatest numbers came between the years 1900-1915. In the following years such groups of workers became a familiar sight throughout the city. According to several sources:

> "Most of them are peasants who came from the southern part of Italy. Upon their arrival here, they were bewildered by the great difference in language, customs and environment. In addition, there was a pressing need for them to earn a living. Naturally they tended to settle with their own group as did most of the early immigrants. Most of them were employed at first, on the fruit farms of James Budlong and John M. Dean."

"Also employed in picking (of strawberries) were large numbers of Knightsville women recently arrived from Italy."

"Their brightly-colored regalia and lusty, light-hearted singing of Old Country songs while they worked was something you'll never see again..."

Another common scene around the year 1905, in Cranston was that of Italian women walking very erect and balancing bundles or baskets on their heads as they went from place to place.

Itri is known for its olives, flour and stone masonry. In Itri, the Itrani had worked primarily in these olive groves which surrounded the Italian mountain village. Generations of Itrani were taught the skills of patient nurturing and timely harvest. In rural Knighsville, with its apples, peach, pear orchards and farmland, the Itrani found an agricultural environment that utilized their skills. The craft skills they acquired in stone masonry industry in Itri were also easily transferred to the cement industry of Knightsville. So, the Itrani picked potatoes, baked bread, and constructed homes and buildings in their new community. The Itrani willingly accepted menial tasks abandoned by Irish and Swedish workers who were stepping up the rungs of labor's ladder. One Itrani woman reminisces about her early years working for John M. Dean, owner of a large apple orchard.

"We all worked on the Dean Farm. I went to work at at John M. Dean Farms when I was twelve years old. I was supposed to go to school, but I left school to work. I had so much responsibility at Dean's estate. All of the immigrants that came to Knightsville came to us for employment. Mr. Dean would ask me if they were friends and would they be good workers. I would respond "Yes, and they need the money." John Dean raised over 45,000 bushels of apples a year. Italians were liked because they were hard workers. They wouldn't only pick apples, they could do anything that was agricultural. They would hoe gardens, pick peaches, grub trees, and anything else that was needed to earn that twelve dollars a week. Mr. Dean liked the Itrani people. I felt proud that being such a young girl, that he would take my advice."

Although most Italian immigrants were unskilled when they settled in Rhode Island, by 1915 comparatively few worked in unskilled labor or construction. The larger numbers found employment in skilled or semi-skilled jobs in foundries, textile plants, the building trades, and jewelry manufacturing firms. Experiencing rapid growth between 1900 and 1930, more than 35 percent of Italian shop keepers during the time owned their own businesses—general stores, clothing stores, and bakeries. Others served the Italian community as independent craftsmen such as barbers, tailors, cobblers, carpenters and tinsmiths. The skilled or professional fields in which the Itrani could be found included medicine, law and dentistry.

RHODE ISLAND ITALIANS IN THE PROFESSIONS

The two fields in which Italian-Americans have made great strides nationally since World War II are education and government; but in Rhode Island they had moved into the power structure of these two fields in significant numbers only since 1960.

With the greatest numbers of Italian immigrants coming to Cranston between the years of 1900-1915, in the appropriate number of years they began to show up in High School Year Books. Whether they worked in the farms or were mill workers, shoemakers, or pushcart peddlers, Italian immigrants worked tirelessly to see to it that their children were educated. This was quite an accomplishment since there were not the advantages of education in their past. Coming from a country where children received three years of education and were expected to work before they reached their teens, they at first, could not understand compulsory education which forced their children to stay in school until well into their teens. Gradually, there became an increasing participation in the educational system as well as change in attitudes towards the school system. A profound respect for the professional is important for Italians. The Itrani desired to have their children educated and became professional or white collar workers. At this they succeeded.

An analysis of the "Cranstonian" yearbook of Cranston High School indicates that the first Italian, became evident in the graduating class of 1930.

That year there were seven graduates with Italian surnames. They were:

Cranston High School-1930-Graduates with Italian Surnames

Filomena Ann Anzenino		Susie Capriano
Norma Castronillani		Mae Filomena DiPanni
Francis Fazzano	Florence Lingo	Henry Mariani

The following years indicated an increase in Italian names as their population increased and the children entered the school system.

YEAR	TOTAL GRADUATES	ITALIAN SURNAMES
1930	109	7
1934	270	25
1940	430	39
1943	344	56
1944	350	64

As for higher education, in January 1919, when Rhode Island College was a teacher training institute, one Italian American woman, Aurelia Declissa Tomassi, received a diploma. The college graduated 4 Italian-American women between the years of 1919-1922. By June 1931, 14 out of a class of 144 graduates of Rhode Island College were Italian American During the depression years, (1934) the percentage of Italian-American graduates declined to a low of 2.3 percent (3 of 127 graduates), Gradually the total rose to 9.2 percent (13 of 141 graduates), in 1939.

The figures did not change significantly until 1960, when 16.4 percent of those receiving bachelor of education degrees (25 of 152) and 19.4 percent of those receiving master of education degrees (7 of 36) were of Italian ancestry. A similar increase occurred during those years at the University of Rhode Island and Providence College. According to the 1980 census, approximately 55 percent of Italian-Americans in Rhode Island are high school graduates and approximately 14 percent have completed four or more years of college.

Over a forty year span, important trends emerge in education. Italian-Americans had begun to assume positions of prominence in education. This is reflected by the growing number of Italian-Americans who held positions as superintendents of public school systems and as principals and supervisors. In 1950 only one Italian was a superintendent of public schools in the state. By 1985, there were eight, including the head of one of the largest school districts; the public school system of Cranston which was led by an Italian-American.

MANUFACTURING

On example of Itrani success in industry is the story of Anthony Saccoccio. Proprietor of Modern Jewelry Casting Company, Anthony was born in Cranston on January 20, 1910, the son of Luigi and Madeline Di Meo Saccoccio. He received his elementary education in the public schools of Cranston and at the age of 12 he began to work in the jewelry factories. There he served his apprenticeship in jewelry tool making. This was followed by experience in the shop and in time he worked himself up to the position of foreman.

In 1931, he went into business for himself by starting a factory where he specialized in bronze molds, a venture in which he has been successful. On May 12, 1936, Mr. Saccoccio married Catherine De Lellis. They became the parents of two children, Louis Anthony and Madeline Anne.

Mr. Saccoccio is a charter member of the Rhody Roller Skating club, the first organization of its kind in the state. He is a member of the City Hall Athletic Club of Cranston.

POLITICAL AFFILIATIONS

The first political affiliation of most first-generation Italians was Republican. There were several reasons for this allegiance. First, the Republicans courted the Italian vote and gave patronage to the Italians by providing them with lower-level municipal jobs. They also pursued national policies like the protective tariff act which made their party appear to be the party of prosperity and party of the "Full Dinner Pail" a widely touted saying of the time. Third, the Yankee-led Republican Party exploited the economic and cultural antagonism that existed between the Italians and the Irish who preceded them in the job market and who were widely Democrats.

During the 1920s a dramatic transformation in the political areas of Rhode Island's Italian-Americans occurred. The transformation from Republican allegiance to Democratic affiliation was prompted by many factors. The Democratic Party began to back much social and economic legislation which benefited workers and consumers. They also sought the elimination of Sunday Blue Laws and other restrictive measures which were opposed by the Italians. On the other hand, the Republican Party was prohibitionists. They also in an attempt to maintain control were immigration restrictive and opposed unionization and pro-union legislation. The decline of the textile industry in Rhode Island and the economic depression had begun to discredit the Republican image as the party of prosperity and the "Full Dinner Pail." In addition, the Republicans had failed to advance Italian-Americans to high public office. At the same time the Irish Democratic Party during the 1920's began to vigorously woo the Italian vote. The party advanced Italian-Americans such as Luigi DiPasquale, running him for Congress in 1920 and making him Democratic State Party Chairman in 1924. In 1932, the Democrats nominated Louis Cappelli for Secretary of State and his victory made him Rhode Island's first Italian-American General Officer. The candidacy in 1928 of Al Smith (who was widely publicized as being part Italian) accelerated the movement of Italian voters towards the Democratic Party. Finally, the social programs of Democrat Franklin Delano Roosevelt and his "New Deal" confirmed the support of Italian-Americans as well as other working-class ethnics. In return for their support, Italians were merited with many influential political offices. In 1945, John O. Pastore became the first Italian-American Governor of any American state. He was elected Lieutenant Governor in 1944 and assumed the office of Governor on October 6, 1945. In 1950, he became the first of his ethnic group to serve in the United States Senate. Pastore became one of the Senate's most powerful, influential, and respected members before retiring from office in 1976.

ITALIANS IN GOVERNMENT

Since that time, Rhode Islanders have elected four more Italian-American Governors; Christopher DelSesto, 1959-1961; John Notte, 1961-1963; Philip Noel, 1973-1977; and Edward d. DiPrete, 1985. As for mayors, there were no Italian-American mayors of Rhode Island cities in 1950. Cranston got its first with the election of James DiPrete; Providence elected its first Italian-American chief executive, Vince A. Cianci, Jr. in 1975. In 1989 five communities in the state had Italian-American mayors; Cranston, Providence, Johnston, North Providence, and Woonsocket.

Since the 1950's Italian-Americans have made a dramatic impact on the government and the judicial system of the state. In 1921 there were only two Italian-Americans serving in the House of Representatives; Benjamin Cianciarulo, born in Italy in 1884. An attorney by profession he was educated in the Providence public schools. The other, Louis V. Jackvony, was born in Providence in 1892. There were none in the state Senate. Ten years later there were eight state representatives, but no senators. By 1940, three of forty-four state senators and nine of one hundred representatives were. The number of Italians in the General Assembly increased marginally during the next thirty years, but the big change did not come until the 1970s. In the 1986 session of the legislature, approximately one-fourth of the members in each house were Italian-Americans.

The Italian-American impact on the state's judiciary has been equally dramatic. In 1922 Antonio Capotosto was named Associate Justice of the State Superior Court. He also served as a Republican-appointed Assistant Attorney General from 1912-1922. In 1935 he was chosen Associate Justice of The State Supreme Court. Also in 1935, Governor Green appointed Luigi DePasquale, as Associate Justice of the Sixth District Court. Nine years later former Secretary of State (1933-1939) and Lieutenant Governor (1941-1944) Louis W. Cappelli, the first Italian to hold general office in Rhode Island, was appointed Associate Justice of the Superior Court. By 1950, there was an Italian-American on the State Supreme Court; Capotosto; one in the Superior Court, Clapelli; one in the District Court, DePasquale; one in Probate Court, Fred Brosco of Johnston; and one in Police Court, Harold Arcaro.

Today, Rhode Island's Italian-American community exerts a tremendous amount of economic, political, and cultural influence upon the state. Its members are well represented in the professions, especially law, education, medicine, the clergy and government. The children of the original immigrants are the doctors, lawyers, teachers, business leaders and politicians of the state today. Local Italian-Americans have also established many civic, fraternal, religious and cultural organizations, including establishing their own newspaper.

L'ECO DEL RHODE ISLAND

L'Eco Del Rhode Island was founded in 1897 by Federico Curzio, whose goal was to "inform and unite" the growing Italian American community of Rhode Island. It was the only Italian American publication of the state. He wanted to serve the needs of the new residents via a newspaper published in the Italian language. Originally published in Italian and printed daily, readers were treated to a variety of news stories and features of interest to its followers. As second and third generation Italian-Americans became increasingly more aware of their heritage and culture, many improvements were made to the existing format. Originally published in Italian and printed daily, it became a weekly newspaper and printed in English. Along the way, the name changed from L'Eco to The Echo, apparently to accommodate a changing readership. The newspaper continued to expand through the years as it came under the ownership of several different publishers. During the 1930's, under the editorship of Antonio Pace, and Italian language pioneer on local radio, the paper grew in size, scope and coverage. Later under the editorship of Doreen Dimitri, the second Italian woman to serve in this post, (the first was Jean Rossi), the paper was written entirely in English. It remained that way so long as Joe Fuoco was editor. He eventually left the paper to establish the bi-lingual Italia U.S.A. As of 1992, the Echo was printed every Thursday and published in Providence. The Echo's last publisher was Richard Baccari, and Editor-in-Chief was Joseph Fuoco. Richard Baccari, as president of the Downing Corporation, was one of many Rhode Island real estate developers of Italian heritage.

Despite the questionable welcome, the Itrani weathered the hostility and made their mark in the harsh, exploitative, paternalistic atmosphere that existed in the Cranston mills and truck farms. They persevered, however. Their strong entrepreneurial spirit led many of them to abandon the status of wage earner and go into business for themselves. They have enjoyed considerable success in the construction trades, jewelry industry, and retail merchandising. By thrift and hard work they earned the money to buy their own homes. They cultivated the land and grew gardens of vegetables, yards of fruit trees, vineyards and flowers. During the 1930's and 1940's, the Itrani flourished. They encouraged the education of their children and made contributions to the community. Their children are the doctors, lawyers, teacher, business owners and politicians of the state today. The Itrani continue to be a strong community who, always mindful of their cooperative struggle, share a sense of trust and unity.

CHAPTER 3

DUE PAESE, UNA TRADIZIONA

The Meaning of Religion For The Itrani

A sufficient body of conflicting literature, both theological as well as sociological has been accumulated regarding the relationship that existed between Italian immigrants and the Catholic Church. While on the one hand, Italian immigrants were portrayed as expressing strongly anticlerical sentiments stemming from their relationship to the church in Italy; the other view presents Catholicism as the strong center of immigrant life. Indeed, at their first stop in the United States on Ellis Island, ninety-five per cent of Italians identified themselves as Roman Catholics. As Italians emigrated to the United States in ever increasing numbers in the later eighteen-hundreds, and the early nineteen hundreds the problem for the Roman Catholic Church grew in proportion, leading to what some theologian researchers have referred to as "the Italian problem". Since the greater number of Italians settled in the large cities, the problem was by far the most acute in these sections and thus more attention was paid to the relationship of the immigrant to Catholicism in metropolitan areas. The question of the relationship of the church and Italian immigrants settling in other areas of the country drew less interest.

Philip Rose, in *The Italians in America*, described the newcomers to America as encountering two religious currents; one tending to fix them in their Roman Catholicism and the other tending to be so thoroughly mired in superstition as to detach them from it. He writes:

> "But they have inherited all the varieties of defective faith and practice which they have at home, such as irregular church attendance anti clerical hostility, and antipathy to religion on the one hand, while bigotry, superstition, and attachment

to religious conventions if not religious realities persist upon the
other."

Continuing with this critical perspective he finds that the difficulties
Italians confronted were of their own making:

> "The chief difficulty has undoubtedly been Italian preju-
> dice against priests, and unfamiliarity with direct contributions
> for church support."

Rose further states that those who were less religious quickly abandoned any pretense that may have existed, once they realized the liberal
atmosphere that existed in America towards religion. These kinds of
observations have been interpreted as a casual or even ambivalent attitude
toward the church and its teachings on the part of the Italian immigrant.
For example, "The Italian takes his religion lightly...he comes to us in
a state of mental and moral reaction...he belongs quite as much to the
army of the unchurched as to the ranks of Catholicism among eighty
Italian newspapers in the United States no one is religious or Catholic."
(The Literary Digest of October 11, 1913, quoting the Catholic Citizen
of Milwaukee.)

CONFRONTING IRISH CATHOLIC TRADITIONS

When those Italian immigrants who were religious and wished to continue their religious practice approached the Catholic Church in their
new country, they were confronted with practices to which they were not
accustomed. Their Catholicism differed from the prevailing Catholicism
which dominated the American Church. The Irish dominated and set
the tone for the American Catholic Church. Irish Catholicism's strict
adherence to the obligations of their religion came into direct conflict
with the Italian Catholic tradition. One of the most notable differences
involved the practice of donating money to the church. Italian Catholic
tradition did not conform to the need for direct financial contributions
for church support from parishioners. Accustomed to a church supported
by the Italian government, the immigrant did not wish to understand
or respond to the necessity for direct financial giving for church maintenance. According to many there seemed to be an obsession with the

American church with raising money, and not with religion. (The Catholic Encyclopedia, Article Italians, p.205)

As late as 1939, the observation was made in the parish of Holy Ghost Church in Providence that Italians:

> "cannot conceive of a priesthood who are continually asking for money and that they are always imposing tasks of collecting funds on those who wish to assist at the divine offices."

The Italian immigrants simply could not understand why they should have to pay money to pray in church. The following is a personal memoir regarding this issue:

> "I can still feel the embarrassment that I personally felt when my own mother would defy the collection box that was placed in full view of mass attendees at Our Lady of The Scapular Church on East 29th Street in New York City. The collection box standing at the entrance has a sign posted which read "Donation for seat---25cents". Two men from the parish, Holy Name Society stood monitoring the box. As the men would scowl at my mother for not paying for her seat, she would scowl back and simply state "people shouldn't have to pay money to pray to God".

Another problem confronted was the differences in the status of women as perceived by the Italian Catholics in the American Catholicism. Italian Catholics experienced relationships to the supernatural in terms of relations to saints and the Madonna rather than to God directly. (Alba). In fact, "A great cult of the Blessed Virgin Mary exists in Italy, where she is called "Madonna" (My Lady), and where she is considered "Mother of All." In a way she typifies the Italian mother, towards whom there is a strong emotional attachment in all Italian families" (Russo, 1970, p.204). The mother of Jesus she is the most celebrated, most venerated and most honored in the naming of Churches and the naming of female babies. She remains one of the compelling Icons of western civilization.

Further tensions revolved around the Irish hierarchy which was unsympathetic toward the Italian faith. The bitterness expressed toward them by the church caught the Italians by surprise and they were unprepared to defend themselves. During the early years there were few Italian priests to serve and represent them. In 1918, there was only one Italian priest for every 5,600 Italian Catholics (Vecoli, 1979, p.266). In addition in most parishes Italian mass was held in the basement of the church, to which they had been consigned in some Irish-American churches. As a result, Italian Americans became what writer Albert Giovanetti called "basement catholics." There existed a sharp distinction between the upper and lower churches. Church attendance was consequently negatively affected by hostile treatment of this kind.

RELIGION FOR THE ITRANI

Religion for the Itrani was a strong unifying force that helped them survive the harsh realities of their new world experiences. Religion was retained by deep and proud roots in Italy, the center of Roman Catholicism. The first Itranis to immigrate to Rhode Island sought to re-create that same sense of strong religious community in the Cranston area. Their purpose was to satisfy the desire to preserve continuity with their past lives in Italy and to find meaning and strength in their immigrant experience in their new country. Through their religion, the network of Itrani became not only a necessary expression of ethnic and religious solidarity, but to a certain degree, a strategy for coping with the larger surrounding society. Although some of the Itrani chose to attend services at the old Saint Rocco's Church, most of the Itrani went to services at the predominantly Irish Saint Ann's Church. When the Itrani first arrived, they too found a catholic church controlled by Irish priests and bishops, who were hostile toward the brand of Catholicism the Italians practiced. To the Irish the religious practices of immigrants were more like those of a folk religion, with a mix of superstitions and worship. The long street processions led by a marching band, with the faithful carrying statues of the Madonna and a whole array of saints laden with dollar bills, followed by praying chanting parishioners holding candles and strewing flower petals along the way seemed more like pagan rituals than Catholic practices to the austere Irish Catholics.

In his classic video, "The Americanization of Itri" photographer Salvatore Mancini addresses the differences in religious practices. He says:

"Imagine Knightsville in the year 1905, a Yankee Village of farms and orchards and textile mills. The first festival must have been quite a sight with its long procession of women, many devotionally barefoot, singing ancient hymns in their native dialect and men carrying their newly commissioned statue of the Madonna on their shoulders. This first celebration served to establish the Itrani as a community. In honoring the Madonna they honored and confirmed their ties to Itri in a special way acknowledging the sacrifices, labors and dreams of their parents and their culture. These Itrani who first had brought Itri and Itri's holy Icon to America in this act, had consecrated Knightsville as their new home."

By 1921, the Italian population numbered more than 3,500 people, outnumbering the Irish, and an "Italian Committee of Cranston" was formed to petition the Diocese to establish their own parish. Leaders of the Itrani community which included Antonio Cardi, Joseph Bellayuto, Luigi Marluzzo, Luigi Vallone, and Antonio Manzo worked diligently towards their goal. In a series of open letters to the Bishop they cited "the neglect that they have been experiencing...the necessity of giving a religious education to their children... and the desire to organize themselves within the customs and needs of the Itrani culture." In an impassioned plea that "we will make any sacrifice providing you deliver us from the present slavery and the continuous persecutions of the American priest against all the Italians..." they requested permission to organize their own parish.

In response to the requests of the Itrani in Cranston, Bishop Hickey assigned an Italian priest, Reverend Cesare Schettini to organize a congregation. Finally in 1925, a new parish was created, and in 1935 construction began on Saint Mary's Church on Cranston Street. The parish and the church were named for the Madonna Della Civita, the patron saint of Itri. Before designing the church, the congregation sent a local architect to study the church in Itri that houses the Madonna, so that the one in Cranston would be an exact duplicate. Although the Itrani today are spread across the city, its spiritual home is Knightsville, and St. Mary's Church on Cranston street.

EVENING FEAST CELEBRATION IN GAZEBO

BUILDING THE CHURCH

The experiences of the Itrani regarding the building of a church were similar to the experiences of other Italian immigrants in various parts of the Untied States. As soon as a community became large enough and prosperous enough to support a church of their own—a church of their preference, one that would fulfill their needs—plans were begun. Thus, the development of the Roman Catholic Church in the United States has paralleled the growth of Italian immigration. In so far as has been possible, the establishment of a Roman Catholic Church has followed every Italian settlement in the United States (Cordasco & Brecchoni, 1974, p. 236).

FATHER CESARE SCHETTINI—ITRANI'S FIRST PASTOR

For the first thirteen years of his service, Father Schettini labored among his people, celebrating two masses each week in the basement of St. Ann's Church. He worked with the Italian committee to achieve their goal of a parish for the Itrani. The Itrani population has surpassed the entire parish family of St. Ann's Church, yet the Bishop did not respond to letters and interviews regarding the establishment of an Italian parish. By January of 1924, the committee purchased eleven lots of the Haven Homestead on Cranston Street as a site for the church. Father Schettini wrote to the Bishop saying "The Italian population of Cranston is full of good spirit, love, respect and trust in their Bishop and are ready to support and sacrifice for the erection of their own institution."

On April 12, 1925, Bishop Hickey created St. Mary's Parish, appointing Father Schettine as pastor. By 1935, the parish had grown to six hundred and seventy-one families composed of more than forty-five hundred people. Sunday school instruction was held in the church. A faculty of twenty-nine teachers directed classes to a total of five hundred and forty-three students. Father Schettini directed that a fund-raising drive for a church be initiated. The economic depression had hit Rhode Island about six years earlier than the rest of the country, yet the people gave generously. Volunteers were organized to canvas the Itrani to solicit contributions for their church. Solicitors were sent out in pairs and each donor was presented a passbook in which his or her regular contribution was listed and acknowledged. Ninety percent of the money in the church fund came from the nickels, dimes and pennies of the people who made the parish the recipient of their savings. This was a remarkable demonstration of solidarity, generosity and the faith of the Itrani, considering it was in the height of the great economic depression.

By early 1935, there was enough money to warrant the beginning of a church. Erminio Migliori, an architect, was sent to Itri to make architectural drawings of the church that housed the precious Maddona. The transplanted Itrani wanted a church that most closely resembled the Itri shrine. Plans called for an edifice of Italian Renaissance style of red brick with limestone trim. The approach to it would be characterized by a broad terrace surmounting a number of steps with bluestone treads and brick risers. Specifications called for the entire building to be fireproof with concrete floor construction. A unique rose window adorned the front wall, above the main entrance. Ground breaking ceremonies took place on Palm Sunday, April 14, 1935; ten years after Father Schettini became pastor. Elaborate ceremonies were held for all parish societies and fraternal, civic organizations. More than fifteen hundred people attended. The festivities included a parade through the principal streets of the parish followed by the traditional turning over of the first sod by Bishop Keough, Father Schettini, Judge Antonio Capotosto, and Maria Figliozzi Cardi, the widow of Antonio Cardi. Many other civic officials were present including the Italian vice Counsel of Providence. The memorable day concluded with benediction of the Most Blessed Sacrament in old St. Ann's Church.

Construction of the magnificent church proceeded at a brisk pace. Within a year, the basement of the new church was completed and first services were held there on April 5, 1936. All shrines and furnishing were removed from old St. Ann's in a solemn observance following the completion of the parish's Lenten mission. Construction of St. Mary's Church occasioned a second round of donations by its parishioners. The main altar, the marble pulpit and two side altars, dedicated respectfully to Our Lady of the Valley and Santa Oliva, were donated by devoted families of the parish. The original communion rail was donated by more than hundreds of parishioners.

At long last, the new church with its capability of over eight hundred was ready for its dedication. Bishop Keough came to the parish on July 3, 1938, to bless the cornerstone and officiate at the ceremonies. The dreams of the Italian committee of seventeen years before had now become a reality. Father Schettini officiated at the first Mass assisted by Reverend Peter Gorret and Reverend Louis D'Aleno.

Music for the ceremony was provided by the St. Peter's parish choir from Warwick, Rhode Island. The dedication ceremonies concluded the following week with a gala testimonial dinner honoring Father Schettini which followed the placing of a statue of Santa Maria over the exterior arch of the church's main entrance.

By the end of 1938, Father Schettini was ministering to more than forty-five hundred parishioners. It was clear that the size of his flock has grown much more than any one priest could handle. This was evident to Bishop Keough at the dedication ceremonies. Thus, on December 3, 1938 he assigned Reverend Oliver J. Bernasconi as assistant pastor.

Father Bernasconi proved to be an invaluable addition. He was given control over the Sunday school program which had greatly expanded to more than seven hundred students. He moderated numerous parish societies which had also grown in membership,. By 1939, there were seventeen active societies in the parish with a combined membership of nearly one thousand people. Father Bernasconi reorganized the Holy Name Society in 1940 and was instrumental in creating interest in the parish and its activities on the part of parish youth. He introduced a varied athletic program; and soon thereafter, the parish baseball team won its division championship.

On June 17, 1945 a dinner was held to honor Father Schettini and to burn the church mortgage. Father shared in the joys of the parish on that day, but knew that there was still much more to be done. At the banquet, he set the tone for the parish's next few years by announcing that the major goal of St. Mary's would be a parish school. The tireless pastor knew that one of the best ways to solidify the parish's future was to build a school for the youth who would become the leaders of tomorrow.

A combination of events, however, prevented the school project from being initiated immediately. The parish celebrated its silver jubilee in 1948, commemorating the struggles and accomplishments of Father Schettini and the Italian committee two and one-half decades earlier. An honored guest at the festivities was the Archbishop-designate of Baltimore, none other than Bishop Keough of Providence, who had supported and shared in so many of the parish's past achievements. Father Schettini reiterated his wish for the initiation of plans for a school and convent at the jubilee ceremonies. Unfortunately, he never saw his dream become a reality. He died March 16, 1951.

Father Bernasconi continued as administrator until 1954 when he was appointed as the second pastor of St. Mary's. Many things happened to the parish in the meantime. The young priest had supervised the refurbishing of the church and rectory in September of 1949. Two months later, Bishop McVinney made his first visit to the parish to officiate at the blessing of the church bells. Father Bernasconi had announced the donation of the bells at the Maddona Festival in July of 1949. The bells' combined weight exceeded one ton and they could be heard sounding the "Angelus" three times daily.

In 1951, land was bought as a proposed site for the new school. A few months later, additional land, both behind the school site and on land which the present convent stands, was donated. A school building fund drive was inaugurated in September of 1952. Simultaneous to the drive, the convent-school opened with a kindergarten of some twenty-eight students. Succeeding years saw the temporary school expand by adding one grade each year until 1954.

The parish corporation voted to expend three hundred thousand dollars for the construction of a new modern school in 1954. Actual work on the school began in March and proceeded at such a brisk pace that it was ready for the 1954-55 academic year with Sister Superior Carmelo Lasco as principal. The school building was designed with the most modern facilities and conveniences available at the time. It contained eight classrooms, a visual aid room, library and gym. Such modern facilities made possible a varied and interesting curriculum including needle craft, phonics, dancing, guitar, typing, various types of art and a comprehensive guidance program.

PARISH ACTIVITIES

The Social activities of St. Mary's Church include the sponsorship of Church societies, a parochial school, Sunday-school instruction and a number of parish societies. Among the most important of the church societies are the following:

The Catholic Youth Organization   St. Ann's Society
Holy Name Society   St. Mary's Society
St. Aloysius Guild   Children of Mary Society
Third Order of St. Francis Chapter   Senior and Junior Choirs
Confraternity of Christian Doctrine   St. Vincent de Paul Conference

The last group was especially important to the Itrani during the depression. It aided many impoverished families of the parish through various works of charity.

ITALIAN SPEAKING SOCIETIES

St. Mary's also has six active Italian Speaking Societies, most of which were founded in the early days of the parish. These societies are:

Societa Parrochiale Maria S.S. Della Civita   Societa Di Sant' Anna

Maria Santissima Della Valle   Pia Unione Di S. Giuseppe

Terze Ordine Di San Francesco   Societa Di Santo Rocco

LETTER FROM ITRI TO AUTHORS MOTHER--1954

Despite the fact that some observers of Italian immigration had maintained that the immigrant expressed an antipathy towards the church organization which they had in Italy and which they brought to the United States, this was not the case with the Itrani. As we see they were neither poor financial supporters of the church, nor anti-clerical. When the Itrani were able to begin their own parish and build their own church they proved to be generous and faithful in the practice of their religion.

THE CIVITA COMMUNITY CENTER

"Guests Only—Authorized Guests Must Be Accompanied By A Member" reads the sign at the Civita Community Center. On any evening, the large community room is full of men, puffing on cigarettes or tiny cigars, talking in Italian, and playing a card game called briscola, (or Italian rummy or scoppa or tre sette). They will be drinking a cup of espresso and nibbling Italian cookies. Every night the club is filled with several dozen men from the Knightsville families who are active members. The Society has a large building near Itri Square and the Gazebo, the site of the annual feast. During the feast, the "Members Only" rule is dropped as festival attendees are allowed access to the private club. A separate "Shrine Room" contains an altar and a painting of La Madonna Della Civita in honor of their patron saint. On an opposite wall are plaques containing the names of all those families who made contributions in 1967 to the "Building Memorial Fund." The Civita Community Center was officially dedicated June 28, 1969.

ITRI CENTER WITH BANNER PROCLAIMING FEAST

For the men of Knightsville, the club takes the place of the piazza in Itri. In the piazza, one sees his friends, talk's politics, transacts business and has a coffee or drink at the café. "For us, this is like the piazza" said

Mr. Sinapi, a tanned man who came to Knightsville in 1966, with, as his own personal legend goes, a bag of sausage in his hands. "If someone says, 'Listen, I need some help' you help them—whether it is to fix a roof, to fix a fence, a brick walk or cement walk. You talk, you help!" The circolo sociale, the social club in Itri, has been transplanted to Knightsville with slight variation from its original form.

An important activity of the community center is the annual feast. In 1905, the Saint Mary's Feast Society was founded under the name "Comitato Festa Di Maria SS Della Civita". Today, this society commonly known as the "Feast Committee" is a well organized, non-profit organization which became state chartered as of May 19, 1966. It continues today as an active society that seeks to maintain the tradition of observing the annual feast in July honoring Madonna SS Della Civita. The entire costs of the feast are paid by this Society. The members are a hard working group that holds monthly planning meetings throughout the year, and run special fund-raising activities to help defray the costs of the feast.

The membership consists of men who were born in Itri, sons and relatives whose ancestry originated in Itri and other Catholic men who have joined to help honor the Madonna SS Della Civita.

SOCIETY PRESIDENTS
MEN
1905-1991
Antonio Di Biase

Antonio Cardi	Enrico Persichino
Albert Cataldi	August Pezza
Dante Ciambrone	Francesco Pezza
Arthur DiSegna	Bambino Ruggieri
Luigi DiSegna	Michael Saccoccia
John Fabrizio	Alexander Saccoccio
Frank J. Manzi	Bambino Schiapo
Joseph Manzi	Louis A. Schiapo
Frank P. Marino	Joseph Schiappa
Carlo Matrullo	Benedict J. Sepe
Luigi Merluzzo	Benny Sinapi

Louis Nardollillo
Frank Paliotti
Pasco Paliotti
Alphonse Tedesco

Antonio Soscia
Clement Soscia
Anthony D'Amore

LADIES AUXILIARY
1967-1988
FIRST PRESIDENT
Josephine Cataldi

Angela Maibon
Mary Hasty
Louise Juskalian
Kathleen T. Manzi

Anna Renzi
Mary Ruggieri
Charlotte Schiapo
Mary St. Jean

THE ROLE OF TRADITION

Tradition is deeply valued in Italian communities, both to honor achievement and to illustrate the general process of immigrant adaptation and ethnic persistence in urban America. Tradition tends to be strongest in old and tightly knit communities and is the culture that is carried from one generation to the next. By keeping up with tradition, we remember where we came from. By repeating what is meaningful we give order to our lives. Great traditions are generally passed on through large institutions such as the school, church, and government. Other traditions are transmitted in more intimate settings such as the family and small social groups.

As many other European peasants, Italian immigrants brought folk customs and beliefs with them. They brought numerous social customs which were perpetuated in the homogeneous communities in which they found themselves. Prominent among the tradition was the honoring of a patron saint and the annual religious festival honoring that saint. Every little village in Italy had at least one patron saint, which was prayed to with candles, novenas, and masses. At times, good deeds were promised if only the saint would grant their favors or intercede with God on their behalf. This protection was counted on by those who came to America. Many of these local saints have become so famous that they have widespread following. Saint Gennaro is one of these. Some saints have specific parts of the body to which they provide aid. For example, Saint Biagio is appealed to for help in the cure of a sore throat, while Saint Lucy is the one to pray to for any illness concerning the eyes. Don Bosco, a recently canonized saint, is credited with particular interest in protecting the young. Two saints, Saint Jude and Saint Rita, considered saints for the hopeless, are the saints to whom those in despair may turn. Saint Anthony of Padua is believed to make thirteen graces a day to God. Prayers are made to him to intercede with God for one of these graces. Many an adult recite the prayer learned as a child when something is lost:

> Saint Anthony, Saint Anthony
> Come around
> There is something lost
> That must be found

According to the devout, within a few minutes that item will be found.

Religious festivals have been celebrated in Italian towns and villages since the middle ages. The roots exist in pre-Christian times. In Italy, a typical festival includes the procession of the statue or shrine through the streets; a mass celebrating the town's patron, feasts, and games. For centuries they have become associated with the worship of patron saints. Some of the original religious celebrations, such as the festival of San Gennaro (the martyred Saint of Naples) on New York City's Lower East Side are still held annually throughout the United States. Every urban American community containing an Italian population celebrates the religious festival honoring their patron Saint; The North End of Boston, Mulberry Street in lower Manhattan, the Hill section of St. Louis, the south side of Philadelphia, the Federal Hill of Providence, the North Beach section of San Francisco, Chicago's near west side. At the church of Our Lady of Mount Carmel in Brooklyn, an "Annual Dance of the Giglio and the Boat" takes place. A traditional highlight of the "Festa" is the 85 foot, four-ton tower that holds a full orchestra and is carried on the shoulders of more than 100 young men and paraded through the streets of the parish. Similarly, an annual feast of "Our Lady of Mount

Carmel takes place in Westerly, Rhode Island. At St. Rocco's church in the Thornton section of Rhode Island, an annual festival honors the patron saint, St. Rocco, the leper saint. In the Silver Lake section of Providence, an annual feast honors the martyr, St. Bartholemew. On Long Island, in New York, such towns as Hicksville, Island Park, Deer Park, Levittown, Massapequa and Glen Cove, the annual religious festival thrives.

La Festa is the social and religious highlight of the year for the community. Angonio Mangano in "The Associated Life of the Italians in New York City" states "It is the custom of each of the small group societies to have an annual festival, and it is in connections with such occasions that the Italian manifests his love for show and pomp, uniforms, banners, music, and elaborate discourse. Eating and drinking are the chief features, and order generally prevails." Feasts provide opportunity for re-establishment of religious ties, sociability, renewal and strengthening of neglected relationships. As a rule, the feasts occur in midsummer, when decorations, street illuminations, fireworks and processions are indulged. Some dress in their colorful native costumes and dance the folk dances of their town or village in Italy. No inducement could tempt the Italian to miss these festivals.

ST. MARY'S FEAST DAY PROCESSION:
A LINK WITH KNIGHTSVILLE'S PAST

For the Itrani, the first known "Festa" in this country followed the celebration of the high mass in St. Rocco's Church on July 21, 1895. The Itrani were jubilant and carried the statue of the Madonna through the streets of Knightsville. The first "Americanized" version of the feast consisted of three pinwheels which were set up by John Soscia. According to documented sources the first feast was described as follows;

> A set schedule of events characterized the ceremonies. On July 20th, at 6:00 a.m. a salute of aerial bomb was fired as a sign of the inauguration of the festivities. A band then would lead a procession to the church where High Mass was held. Following this service, the figure of the Madonna was carried from the church to the parish grounds where it received a specially made crown. A procession then followed starting from the church and marching down the principal streets of the

parish. The procession was easily recognizable by the presence of the "chanters," a group of women from St. Mary's Society who chanted Italian hymns of worship to let all know that the Madonna was close behind them. Men bid as high as one hundred dollars for the privilege of carrying the Madonna in the procession. As the figure passed, people would make an offering by pinning paper money onto it or by laying Gold or silver necklaces on the statue. Coin offerings could also` be given by depositing them in a box carried immediately in front of the Madonna. At times, worshipers followed the image along the hot July pavement barefoot as a sign of penance and as an act of thanksgiving for favors received. After the procession, family dinners were held. During the feast the parishioners open their homes and provide lavish spreads of good food and wine. Family members, friends and neighbors were all welcomed. Many groups gathered outdoors beneath the grape arbors and celebrated far into the evening. The size and scope of the ceremony seemed to grow larger and better each year, particularly after the founding of St. Mary's Parish.

Today, the feast continues to be a visible expression of the religious fervor of the Italian American community. The rhythm of any community can be measured by the time, energy and resources given to the preparation of the feast as well as the celebration of the event. While it is true that some of the feasts in other localities appear to bear little resemblance to an event meant to honor a patron saint and are described by some as "Italian Fairs", the Itrani have continued to center La Festa on a solemn expression of religion. It is a sacred time of year for the Knightsville community.

After months of preparation and meeting, it is time. The festival begins at St. Mary's Church during the week prior to the actual feast day, with a five-day celebration of Novenas in honor of Maria SS Della Civita. On the Friday night of the feast week, an open-air mass is held for all in the community to attend. Following the Mass there is a candlelight procession through the streets of Knightsville, during which the Holy Rosary is recited by both priests and participants. The participants of the procession chant "The Stornelli" in the traditional Neapolitan dialect, the dialect of the paese in a chant:

FEAST PROCESSION ASSEMBLING IN FRONT OF ST. MARY'S CHURCH IN KNIGHTSVILLE

INNO TRADIZINALE ITRANO
(RICONSTRUITA DA ITALIA FABRIZIO IN SINAPI)

I

Madonna della Civita Benedetta
Che stai coppa su monte Sola Sola
Ho Benedetta
E Munsignore ti venne a visitare
Mamma Maria Ulimm Incoronare'
Na Coronella d'oro te Ulim mette
Ma centrellata co centrelle c'ore

A Bash L'annunziata te Ulim purtane
E Contisposta Agliutare Ma ggiore
A le ci corse Ron Angelo De Fabritus
Con tutta la, Signoria della casa

Che Bella Signorina che sta a Itri
Davanti alla Madonna Aggianichiata

Ho gente di Gaeta, che colete or bulete se la
Madonna cu hoi non ci ho voluto stane

II

Ho voluto venire a questa terra D'Itri
Per dare Onore a voi Shellerati
Glii regn all' a Campagna e' correva
E Munsignore le rette La Benedizione

Ammen a consi sia Madonna Mia
Ti sia raccomandata quest'anima mia
L'anima di mio Padre e della mia Madre
E di tutta quanta la Christianitane
E di mia Madre

E di tutti quanti chi male e bene
Ci vuole

Friends and relatives come together in a sense of togetherness as they participate in the sharing of prayer and candle lighting. The solemnity continues throughout the weekend, ending with the High Mass on Sunday morning. After the Solemn Mass, the Madonna is carried down the church steps into the streets of Knightsville. Here she is mounted on wooden stretches and carried on the shoulders of sweating, but proud and happy devotees in a solemn procession. The carriers have religious medals, badges and buttons on their jackets with bright sashes with shiny letters honoring La Madonna. This is the highlight of the day for carriers and viewers. The Madonna is carried in glory. The congregation falls in behind the procession carrying candles and chanting prayers. Immediately following the Madonna come the Verginelle (the little virgins), young girls all dressed in white wearing fine white veils, symbolic of the Madonna's virginity. The various church societies and sodalities join in solemn procession carrying banners. The local drum and bugle corps of uniformed musicians follow and play music. The procession circulates through the streets past the great vine covered atrium with its Corinthian columns near Itri Square, where the map of Itri is carved in the sidewalk. During this procession devotees may pin donations on her dress out of respect and perhaps gratitude for some past blessing. The figure of the seated Virgin Mary, the crown on her head and the child sitting on her lap, her arms raised upwards and open, is one of the oldest images of the Itrani. The streets are decorated with elaborately colored lights; red, white and green streamers, Italian and American flags fly side by side, all marking the route of the procession and celebrating the coming of the saint. Along the route, tables are set up where the Madonna can rest, and flower petals are strewn at her feet. Knightsville residents waiting on their front steps can then come out and meet La Madonna and greet their neighbors in celebration. Others caress the statue in order to receive the sacred power of the Saint. Members of the Feast Society accompany the statue distributing key chains and medals with the image of La Madonna. Laden with donations, the statue is returned to the church as the priests offer a final benediction and the Madonna returns to her niche inside the church.

The fundraising carnival usually held in the evening has rides for the children, games of chance for the adults, and foods and pastries made by local businesses, parish groups or civic organizations. The gaily decorated booths may sell veal scallopine and sausage and pepper sandwiches, pizza, beer and wine, cotton candy and a local favorite, the doughboy (a deep-fried pastry, similar to the zeppolli, sprinkled with confectioner's sugar). Other stands will hold "I dolci" or pastry of all kinds, torrone (Italian taffy filled with hazelnuts); shelled nuts strung up and hanging, and Italian torta.

In the evening music is provided by concert bands in the Gazebo of Itri Square. The musicians sit on a platform decorated with colored lights and flags. The band plays popular tunes, selections from operas, patriotic melodies, and songs. At midnight, there is a fireworks display. Private homes are open at night, and under the grape arbors in the yards near the backyard shrines honoring La Madonna, Itranis sit and eat and talk, renewing social ties.

Many others stroll down to the gazebo in the center of Knightsville to listen to the music. On this feast weekend, Knightsville is filled to capacity with more than 50,000 pilgrims who come from near and far to pay homage to the Madonna in remembrance of the vision of Mary upon Civita Mountain in Itri.

BACKYARD SHRINE TO MARIA SS. DELLA CIVITA IN KNIGHTSVILLE

Through the years second and third-genera-tion Itrani have continued the St. Mary's Day tradition with little varia-tion. In the spirit of exchange, a group of Cranston Itrani goes annually to Itri to celebrate the Feast of the Madonna firsthand, and the Parish Priest from Itri comes to Cranston to celebrate the feast there.

THE LEGEND OF THE BELOVED
MADONNA SS DELLA CIVITA

The legend of the Madonna Della Civita is one of the most fascinating religious histories ever told, of a devotion which began 2,000 years ago and has endured through the centuries. According to this legend;

> The holy image of the Madonna Della Civita was attrib-
> uted to Saint Luke, the Apostle of Antioch. St. Luke who was
> in communication with the Blessed Virgin, sought to paint
> an image of her with the Christ Child. After completing the
> painting, St. Luke presented it to the Virgin Mother Mary, who
> was very pleased. The Virgin Mary then promised her specific
> protection to all mankind who would possess and venerate the
> special painting. The holy image was then brought forth to the
> world. St. Luke, as the tradition tells, donated it to his native
> city, Antioch, in Syria. St. Pulcheria (399-453) had a temple
> built to house the painting in Constantinople which is now
> Istanbul, Turkey. The temple was under the guardianship of
> the Basilian Monks who protected the treasure. In the Eigth
> Century, during the empire of Leone Isaurico, when the Turks
> captured Constantinople, a crusade was proclaimed against
> the cult of images. Consequently, they destroyed all of the
> churches together with contents. Two elderly monks in their
> deep devotion to Our Lady, sought to protect the precious image
> by enclosing it in a large, wooden chest. They had planned to
> set the chest containing the oil painting adrift at the shore of
> Constantinople, but were discovered by Moslem soldiers. The
> soldiers believing that the chest contained possible treasures
> opened it. When they discovered that it contained only a
> "board", they became angry. They encased the two monks in
> the chest along with the oil painting and threw it into the sea.
> The wooden chest along with its cargo was seen off the coast
> of Sicily, but as the fishermen approached it, as the Legend
> states, the crate moved away from them. They were not the
> chosen people and could not be blessed with the Madonna.
> According to this legend, after floating about for fifty-four
> days and 750 miles, the chest was discovered at the foot of
> Mt. Taurus, Cilica (Asia Minor). When the inhabitants tried to
> pick up the box, they had no difficulty. The monks, were still
> alive and thought they had been in the box for only one day.
> There was, undoubtedly, some mysterious power connected
> with the painting, so it was carried with solemn pomp to the
> largest Church in Ithaca and became very much venerated.
> At the Time Cilicia and all Asia Minor were occupied by the
> Moslems, who profaned temples and worship. The sacred image
> was brought to Messina, Sicily. The people there revered their
> new found treasure and placed it in a church to be venerated.
> They placed the image in a church, where another image, "Our

Lady Of The Letter" was venerated. The merchants of Messina, who were trading with the Orient, asserted that this image was the same which they had heard about when they were in Constantinople. Several hundred years later, the image was found in Gaeta and because the people there did not honor her, the oil painting of the Madonna was taken through a passage in the mountains to Mt. Civita. The next day, the painting was found missing. According to legend the date was July 21, 796, and a deaf and mute herdsman from the town of Itri, while attending his herd of oxen, had observed that a particular ox would continuously wander away from the rest of herd each day and then return. One day, the mute herdsman decided to follow this particular ox. From a distance he noticed that this ox wandered under a holm oak tree. He noticed that the ox kneeled on the ground and gazed into its branches. When the mute herdsman arrived at this site, he also gazed into the branches. He was shocked to see a holy image of the Blessed Mother and Christ Child painted on a board that was encircled by a halo. At this moment, the mute became instantly cured. As his eyes filled with tears of joy, he fell on his knees and meditated for a long time. The painting was the one attributed to Saint Luke. After meditating, the cured herdsman ran to his hut and poured some oil into a wooden cup and made a lamp which he immediately placed under the sacred image. On the following day, he came down from the mountain and related the detail of his miraculous adventure, to the townspeople of Itri. At first, the townspeople were unwilling to believe the story of the herdsman, however, the residents of Itri recognized the image of the painting attributed to St. Luke. The people removed the the image from the holm oak and carried it to Itri, exposing it to the veneration of the public in the church of St. Francis. On the following day, however, it was no longer in the church. The people were dismayed and set out in search of the image. They finally found it at the same location of the Apparition of the herdsman. It was clearly seen then, that the Virgin preferred the peaceful solitude of the mountain than the noise of the city. They immediately built a hut around the tree to protect the the image from the elements. It is on this site that the Sanctuary Of the Madonna della Civita was built and stands today. The first chapel was built in 950 by the Benedictine Monk of the Monastery of Figline. The faithful of Itri, spared neither gold nor labor in helping build this chapel. In the year 1400, a church was built to accommodate the increasing number of visitors to the chapel. Finally on May

27, 1820, the construction of the present church was begun. The architect was Silvestro De Donatis. Thus, between the years 950 and 1849, several churches were built to house the Madonna. Each was larger to accommodate the crowds that flocked to see the image and pay it homage.

In 1527, the village of Itri suffered from a widespread plague which caused many illnesses and deaths. The townspeople from Itri, prayed for the intercession of the Madonna to her son, Jesus, to rid the town of this deadly plague. They carried the holy image through the town of Itri among the suffering people and through the black mist that covered the town. A short time later, the town was rid of the deadly plague. The Madonna was credited with purging the town of this plague.

Pope Pius VII was petitioned by the people of Itri to allow them the privilege of crowning the Madonna, which he did. Pope Pius VII issued a decree on the 30th day of January, 1777 that the coronation of the virgin of Mt. Civita would take place in Itri that year. The first coronation took place in the sanctuary, on Mount Civita, Itri on July 21, 1777. Great ceremonies characterized the coronation celebration. After the ceremony, the image was removed from the altar and borne in triumph throughout the town. Itri was overflowing with visitors. Festivities were reported to continue for a full week and the day of July 21st became a permanent day of veneration. Thereafter, every year on that day, a celebration is held in Itri. With only minor changes the feast activities continue for ten days. Itrani hands down, from generation to generation, the love, and adoration for their beloved Madonna and gratitude for putting an end to the plague that ravaged Itri. Sweet sounds of melodious voices of the devoted uttering their prayers and songs towards the heavens, glorifying their Virgin Mary permeate the surrounding area. The feast begins with a Holy Mass and ends with the Icon appearing at the top of the flight of stairs that lead down to Piazzale Don Lidio Borgese on the shoulders of loyal people of Itri. The rejoicing population explodes into a rousing ovation. The carriers are followed by groups of women and children who sing hymns and ancient chants. There are young girls dressed as angels, children and elderly women wearing ancient Itri costumes; with a horseman wearing an epoch uniform leading the procession. Following are multi-colored, and numerous groups of emigrants who came just for the occasion from the United States and Canada. Canada which has a large Itrani community in Toronto sends many of their citizens who happily wave their Canadian flags while escorting the Image. There are thousands of observers who crowd the large square to follow the parade. La Madonna is carried through the streets to a flowered throne which serves as a temporary altar which has been prepared outdoors for the opening ceremony. The provincial Passionist Superior Father along with the Rector and other members of the confraternity officiate at the Eucharistic outdoor opening celebration. The procession is followed by the Mayor of Itri and representatives of the Campodimele municipality from the town council of Itri and local police officers. At the conclusion of the opening ceremony, hymns and invocations for grace, the Holy Icon is paraded once again through the streets of Itri and placed on the throne in the church of S. Maria Maggiore. On the following days, prayer vigils are held with mothers, widows, widowers and with the elderly and the young. Other ceremonies are held for the sick, visiting them and giving communion to the invalid. Two feast days are dedicated to the young who had just been confirmed and to those who had just taken their first Holy Communion. These are followed by another three days of the Image of the Madonna of the Civita beginning her journey in procession through the streets of Itri, each day having a different itinerary.

The social events surrounding the feast days are varied. There are different types of musical shows including band concerts, folk group presentations; musical shows for classical and pop music and symphonic concerts appearing in the gazebo. There are also the usual food booths and souvenirs sellers that are found at all feasts. The last night also has a spectacular fireworks celebration to note the end of the feast activities.

One of the most beautiful pages in the history of the Sanctuary of Civita, was the visit of Pope Pius IX (1846-1878) in the year 1849. Prior to 1870, Rome was not united to Italy, and the Roman state was governed by the Papacy. During the years 1848-1849, revolutionary uprisings broke out in the Eternal City. The Pope was forced to seek refuge at Gaeta, a large land and naval fortress which was at the time considered to be in the kingdom of Naples. The sovereign, Ferdinand II, offered his Holiness his royal palace at Gaeta. From Gaeta, the Pope was able to view the sanctuary of Mount Civita. When the Pope was visited by a delegation from the town of Itri, they invited him to visit the Holy Sanctuary. Pope Pius IX accepted the invitation and promised that he would go to the Sanctuary on a Holy Visit, which was set up for the 10th of February, 1849.

On the morning of February 10, a procession of pilgrims departed from the city of Gaeta to render solemn homage to the Madonna. The Pope led the procession, accompanied by the King and Queen of Naples, the Cardinal Antonelli, Monsignor Borromeo and an escort of royal princes, generals, bishops and other high officials. At Itri, the people then visited the Church of the Annunciation, took holy water, and offered incense to the Sacrament, blessing the people. The Pope then led the procession up the winding path of Mount Civita to the Sanctuary. He rode a horse that had stirrups which were trimmed with white satin and gold trappings. He was followed by the faithful. As soon as he arrived at the Sanctuary, the Pope kissed the threshold, and was followed by the royal family and the faithful. The Pope celebrated Mass and administered the Holy Eucharist to all present.

After the mass, the Pope wished to view the painting of The Madonna more closely. He reportedly remained in silent meditation for hours. It has been said that his Holiness Pope Pius IX, because of this visit, had filled his heart with courage and inspiration and conceived of the Idea of the Dogma. After five years, because of this visit and inspiration received, Pope Pius IX in the Consistory (Assemblance of Cardinals in Council around the Pope), on the 8th day of December 1854, proclaimed "Mary Conceived Without Sin."

On his visit, the Pope donated to the Sanctuary the chalice with which he had celebrated the Mass, ten gold pieces, and to glorify the Sanctuary, he wrote these holy words: "Gloriosa Dicta Sunt De Te, Civitas Dei". (Glorious words have been said of thee, City of God). These sacred words

COUSIN VALERIA PREPARING FRESH PASTA

now appear above the altars of the Sanctuary in Itri, the Santa Maria SS Della Civita Church and St. Mary's Feast Society's Madonna Della Civita Shrine Room. The royal family likewise, gave gifts to the Madonna, and the street which leads from Itri to the Sanctuary was built at the expense of the same King, Ferdinand.

On July 21, 1877, the second coronation of the Madonna, took place amid the same celebration as one hundred years prior. During the ensuing years people from all over the world have made pilgrimages to this shrine where the lame, blind, and sickly are said to be cured. The number of miracles performed by The Madonna is so many in number that a special room has been set aside in the Sanctuary. The Room of Miracles located in a monastery on the mountain site of the Madonna's discovery, is a museum documenting numerous ex-voto miracles performed by the Madonna. The room is filled to capacity with discarded crutches, locks of hair, and paintings documenting and commemorating the intercession of the Madonna in desperate, seemingly hopeless situation. Many of the paintings depict American soldiers and sailors, along with their jeeps and ships. In this same room is also the treasure which contains numerous objects of gold and silver; gifts offered to the Madonna for graces received and miracles performed. The sanctuary continues to be visited annually by millions of faithful Christians from all over the world.

Today, the Sanctuary has a most beautiful church with a characteristic Belfry and Ancient Clock that rings the tune of Lourdes "Ave Maria" on off hours. The upper part of the façade, in the Renaissance style, is covered with sculptured Travertine stone, the work of Professor Adolfo Rollo of Bari. The portico, as well as the facade, was restored according to the architectural plans of Lawrence Cesanelli of The Art School of Rome in 1960. The House of Pilgrims at the Sanctuary is dedicated to Don Louis Guanella, whose order, "The Servite Fathers of Charity for Men and the Daughters of Saint Mary of Providence for Women", has maintained the upkeep of the Sanctuary since 1947.

• •

In the late eighteen hundred, colonists from Itri, a village situated in the Appenine Mountains, 50 miles northwest of Naples, desired to continue the traditional festivities to honor the Madonna Ss Della Civita in the United States. Although these newly arrived Italians brought few material possessions with them, they did possess a deep-seated faith and devotion to their Madonna. The first known tribute to the Madonna to be held in this country on her holy day of July 21st was a high mass celebrated in the old St. Rocco's Church in the Thornton area of Cranston. This was approximately in the year 1895. Three years later, a committee was formed by these immigrants to arrange for the first feast celebration. However, it would take another twenty-eight years before the parish of St. Mary's would be formed and authorized to use the basement of St. Ann's Church for its services; and thirty-eight years before ground was broken for their own church, a church that would most closely resemble their beloved Sanctuary on Mt. Civita in Itri.

• •

PORTRAIT OF LA MADONNA MARIA SS DELLA CIVITA

ITALIAN AND ITALIAN AMERICAN FAMILY ENJOYING DINNER DURING FEAST IN ITRI - 1999

FEAST PROCESSION IN ITRI

SHOPPING FOR FEAST AT OPEN AIR FOOD MARKET IN ITRI

IL PRIMO MIRACOLO A ITRI

ANNO 796 D.C.

Nell'allora villaggio D'Itri
Viveva un sordo muto;
Era Giovane, bello e forte
Da nascita, L'udito e la favella non aveva avuto
Il Pastore era la sua professione
In mezzo a tante mucche felice si sentiva;
Della volte non faceva nenmeno colazione
Per andare in cerca della mucca che lui preferiva
Quella mucca era D'avvero tanto bella
Che bel pelo lucente, che sguardo intelligente;
Era come il padrone, gli mancava solo la favella
Pero' ogni tanto si smarriva, ma tornava il d'seguente

Ma un giorno la bella mucca non si ritiro'
Era di luglio che caldo faceva;
Il sordo muto si disperava, Dio Mio!! Ora come faro'?
Senza la sua bella mucca sembrava che piu' niente aveva
Ma dove si sara' smarrita?! Lui pensava.
Forse lagiiu', O lassu', Il Papa' capir gli faceva;
Tutto intorno fin su' la vetta lui guardava
Ma la sua cara mucca non si vedeva
Io vado a valle! Il papa' gli fece capire
"Tu sei agile e forte, vai su la montagna."
In cammin si mise senaza due volte farselo dire
Di tanto in tanto dava uno sguardo diu' nealla campagna
Ma ninente, la sua muca non si vedeva
Di qua' niente, di la' niente, andava sempre piu' in su';
Che caldo! Il sudor d'appertutto scorreva
Si sentiva molto stanco, non c'e' la faceva piu
Ando' fin su' per guarder dall'altro lato
Ormai era proprio in cima alla venta;
Si sedette un po' per prendere fiato'
Ma I suoi occhi frugavano intorno infretta, infretta
Salzo' per veder se dall'altro lato qualcosa si vedeva
Ma su' d'unelce una luce vide brillare;
Cos'era quell baglior di luce lui non sapeva
Tanti pensier faceva ma non sapeva cosa fare
Sara' il sole?! Tra se pensava
Ma no!! Il sole e gia' tramontato;
Dio Mio! Cosa sara? Ma tra se coraggio si dava
E ando' dritto verso quell'albero illuminato
Oh! Che gioia, oh!! Che sorpresa!
La mucca era la inginocchiata;
Con gli occhi fissi e con la testa teas
Guardava in su' come se fosse incantesimata
Anche lui guardo' in aldo un po' timoroso'
La su quell'elce immezzo a quella luce
V'era un quadro tanto meraviglioso
Di colpo si senti rabbrividire

La sua bocca incomincio' a balbettare;
Nemmeno lui capiva cosa stava a dire
Per la prima volta senti' il vento soffiare
Singinocchio' di colpo e incomincio' a pregare
Questo e' un miracolo che ho ricevuto io
A tutti voglio andare a raccontare
Che qui sull'elce c'e' la madre di dio
Tutto tremante dalla gioia incommincio' a chiamare
Oooo taaa....oooo taaa! La mucca l'ho trovara;
Il papa' che sapeva suo figlio non parlava
Peso non diete a quella chiamata
Ma quando vide il figlio con la mucca avanti
E che di nuovo si senti' chiamare
Corse verso lui invoccando tutti I santi
"E un miracolo, mio figlio lo sento parlare"
Tutto racconto' di cio' che aveva visto lassu'
Il suo papa' ascoltava e piangeva,
"figlio mio, cio' che hai visto e la mamma di gesu'
Dopo poche ore del gran miracolo ognuno sapeva
Da ogni parte la gente giungeva
Con amore la Madonna venne lodata;
Ogni giorno molte grazie faceva
Maria Santissina Della Civita venne chiamata
Su quell monte fu' erretta una chiesa
Ove ognuno va' a pregare con fede;
Su da quell monte lei protegge Itri paese
Il cui fu' Benedetto anche dal Capo Della S. Sede

Scritta da Francesco A. Cannella
In onore del Biocentenario Dell'Incoronazione di Maria SS Della Civita

DIRECTIONAL SIGN AT SANTUARIO ON MT. ITRI

CHAPTER 4
NOTABLES FROM ITRI
AND VICINITY

This chapter introduces us to some of the more notable characters or events linked to Itri and some of its neighboring villages. The history of a territory is not only that of military monuments, religious and civic statues, it is also the story of the people who were born there. In terms of notable persons, there were many who have honored Itri and subsequently Knightsville. Some of them are included below.

GIACOMO VIS

Giacomo's first office was as Bishop of Ischia. Later he was ordained as Archbishop of Otranto. In 1376, Pope Gregorio XI, nominated him as Patriarch of Constantinople and two years later, in Fondi, appointed him Cardinale di S. Prassede. As a result of this assignment, Itri, his home town fell under his authority. This was a fortunate event for Itri, as his concern and love for his village, carried great weight with those above him. He used his friendships with local noble families such as the Sferra Family, to grant favors for his beloved Itri. Giacomo died in 1387.

GIOVANNI B. MANZI

Giovanni was born in Itri on March 9, 1831, of Dottore Sisto and Gaetana Pennacchia. An astronomer and scientist he taught math and Physics at College Alberoni di Piacenza, and for many years he was the Superior at the college. He was the founder of the astronomical observatory at the college, an expert meterologist; he was one of the astronomy pioneers in Italy. For his experiments and for his inventions, the famous mathematician was most appreciated by students and colleagues in the world of science and meterology. On the occasion of his fiftieth anniversary of teaching at the College, his students and friends established a memorial, a marble bust of his image. Manzi died in the Castle of Stratto, which he inherited from the Counte Francesco Caracciolo, surrounded by his brothers on July 13, 1912.

FRA DIAVOLO-MICHELE PEZZA

It is difficult to capture the essence of Fra Diavolo, a personality, that much as been written about, both reality and myth. Still today, 232 years after his birth, the Itrani remembers and exalts one of their heroes. But, according to some stories, he was not a hero, but a bloodthirsty brigante. Which is the real Fra Diavolo? Michele Pezza (1771-1806) born in Itri on April 7, 1771, of Francesco and Arcangela Matrullo, was a sickly child. A grave illness threatened the life of little Michele and his mother made a novena to S. Francesco di Paolo begging intercession for the health of the baby. She received his blessing, and in gratitude the child put on the habit of the Francescan order. Because of this his friends and neighbors called him, Brother Michele Arcangelo, which was quickly transformed by a school teacher to Fra Diavolo because of his behavior in school. As a young man, Michele worked hard, but in a situation of defending his honor, he murdered Eleuterio Agresti and his brother. At that point it is said, he became stained or "macchiada" . Subsequently, he formed a band of guerrilla, who was guarding a harsh zone of territory along the Via Appia, where many soldiers were murdered. Fredinando IV could not liberate that territory from the deaths that occurred in the 13 years of military service to his regiments. Michele Pezza helped fight that battle and at that moment was transformed from bandit to soldier. Pezze became a military officer for Cardinal Ruffo in the Anti-French action in Calabria and Naples in 1799 and was greatly admired by the Queen Maria Carolina. He earned this acknowledgement for his intelligent, daring action of guerrilla warfare against the French, who were greatly feared. Strongly opposed to the presence of the French (or more precisely of the Napoleonic troops) in the Kingdom of Naples, he waged a spectacular, bloody guerilla war against the foreign oppressor.

In 1806 he hindered the advance of the French at Gaeta and was largely responsible for the restoration of Ferdinand of Bourbon. Pezza led an adventurous life as the leader of a band of briganti who participated in uprisings against the throne in Naples, both French and Spanish via guerilla warfare. Nicknamed Fra Diavolo-or brother of the Devil-he and his band held uncontested control over a wide area north of Naples from Gaeta. According to legend, he could only be killed by a gold bullet, because he carried a magical amulet, the dried head of a viper in a silk purse under his arm.

Pezza was promoted to the rank of Colonel and invested with the title of Duke of Cassano, for his courage and perseverance in that action. At the end of 1806 the newly promoted Colonel fell into the hands of another Colonel, father of four-year-old Victor, the future General Hugo. Fra Diavolo was taken prison and hung. It was reported that in Palermo, Ferdinand King of Naples, who had taken refuge in Sicily solemnly wore mourning for his Devil. Pezza became both a hero and a martyr to his people. So great and enduring was his legend that his house "La Casa di Fra Diavolo" still stands in Itri as La Guardia Municipale.

In addition, his life inspired an opera written by the French composer, Daniel F.E. Auber in 1830 entitled, "Fra Diavolo Ou L'Hostellerie A' Terracina." The opera ran for almost nine hundred performances at the Opera-Comique, some of them spilling over into the 20th century. Fernand Francelli was the last to play the part of the handsome, rakish bandit. The popularity of Fra Diavolo continued to the era of 78 rpm records and can be heard today on compact disc. Although the opera portrays Pezza as romanesque and romantic, in reality he was described as rather bloodthirsty, and quite appropriately called a demon. His men were Sanfedisti-fellow companions bound by neither religion, nor law; true bandits who often engaged in brutal attacks upon the French troops. Incurable Gallic light-heartedness it is said inevitably turned this rather terrifying figure into a beloved bandit. His name and his character as a well-mannered rascal, or gentleman-thief, were appealing. The Opera's love story of Fra Diavolo was a bourgeois affair between an inn-keeper's daughter and a low-ranking guardsman, with bravery and dash surrounding the story. Fra Diavolo as the Marquis of San Mareco is an odd fellow traveling in a carriage, flirting with the titled English lady he is about to rob, while singing the praises of his splendid life as a bandit and laying claim to a robber's kingdom. Auber's librettist, Scribe apparently cared little for the true story of Fra Diavolo the warrior for the partisan, but bandits were fashionable in the opera world of the 1830's.

Later in 1933, in a spoof of the eighteenth-century Italian opera by Auber, Laurel and Hardy starred in an immensely popular film entitled, "The Devil's Brother". In the film, Laurel and Hardy, as two bumbling brothers, are reluctant bandits in a Hollywood Inn which Fra Diavolo was operating.

HENRY DE TONTI—THE ITALIAN "FATHER OF ARKANSAS"

MICHELE PEZZA ALSO KNOWN AS FRA DIAVOLO

Tonti, son of a banker in exile was born Enrico Tonti in Gaeta in 1674. Lorenzo, his father became a leader in the Neapolitan rebellion against Spanish domination. The revolt was initially successful but the new government was short lived. The banker-turned-rebel escaped to Paris. Young Henry joined the French army as a cadet at the age of 18. From age 18, his whole life was a career of military service for France. At the age of 26 he reached the rank of captain. While fighting the Spanish in Sicily, a grenade shot tore away his right hand. The young captain cut the mangled flesh from his writ, bound the wound and kept fighting. Later a metal hand was fashioned which he wore covered by a leather glove. He became known as the "Man with the Iron Hand."

At 26, Tonti completed his military service and was looking for new adventures. He enlisted for duty in the New World, as a Lieutenant under the French explorer LaSalle. LaSalle had the dream of finding the Northwest Passage to China. The fruitless search had taken him to the Mississippi River which had been explored by other Frenchmen but only as far as Arkansas. LaSalle resolved to explore further and find the mouth of the great river. It was his purpose to travel the full length of the Mississippi River from the Great Lakes down to the Gulf of Mexico and claim it all for the King of France. To pay for this venture the fur trade had to be exploited and means of transportation had to be devised. Thus, Tonti built the first crude sailing vessel to sail on the Great Lakes. He built forts along the Mississippi and gained, from the French King, the fur trading rights in the new territory. On his first Christmas Eve in the New World, Tonti left Fort Frontenac with LaSalle to build a fort on the Niagara River. He braved the dangers of the wilderness to travel across the Great Lakes and then journeyed with LaSalle, down the length of the mighty Mississippi to its delta where it empties into the Gulf of Mexico. Tonti and LaSalle took possession in the name of Louis, King of France and named the southern section "Louisiana" after the King. Tonti and LaSalle erected a column at the mouth of the Mississippi River in 1682, claiming the territory for France. Despite mutinies, hostile Indian tribes, desertion, disease, and damaged or lost vessels, and the assassination of Robert Sieru de LaSalle at age forty-three, Tonti returned to Ft. St. Louis and in he following years continued to govern and guide French destiny. Because of the great respect that the Indians had for Tonti he was able to establish the great Indian confederacy, the only peaceful, law-abiding combination of Indian tribes that ever existed on the American conti-nent. After 1680, he lived in the Mississippi Valley. For 26 years in the savage wilderness, the one-handed but indestructible Tonti had escaped scalping and burning—escaped knives, musket shots and arrows, but starving and freezing he couldn't escape yellow fever. He succumbed to the fever and died September 6, 1704. He had built a fort and set up a trading post at the Arkansas River. Hence, Tonti is sometimes called the "father of Arkansas."

JOHN FUSCO—GAETA/ITRI OLIVE COMPANY

When John Fusco graduated from Hampshire College in Amherst, Mas-sachusetts, he set out for his father's ancestral home, Itri. "I didn't speak a word of Italian," he said, "but within two days of graduation, I was picking olives with my cousins."

Itri has been famous since Roman times for top-quality olives and olive oil. Mr. Fusco was distressed to find that Itri's high-grade, low-acid oil was being sold cheaply in bulk to producers who blended it with lesser oils to bring the total acidity level down to the 1 percent or less required for the extra-virgin qualifications.

Concerned at how little financial return the olive growers were making, and anxious to halt the abandonment of their olive groves, Mr. Fusco convinced his relatives to produce and bottle their own oil under the label, Gaeta Itri. A light, fruity oil with a pale, yellow-green color, Gaeta Itri is available at Macy's Cellar and at all specialty food shops. Mr. Fusco also sells Gaeta Itri olives in bulk and in jars. The olives are small and tender, with a rich smooth flavor that is delicately salty. A beautiful, pale, purple-brown color, they look like little burnished beach pebbles.

Mr. Fusco and his sister, Deborah, recommend a family recipe for using the olives and oil in a way that brings out the full flavor of both. They chop the pitted olives together with a little sweet onion, fresh ripe tomatoes, parsley, mozzarella and basil. Add a few turns of freshly ground black pepper, and mix the ingredients together to make a coarse paste. Rounds of crusty Italian bread, sprinkled with a few drops of water to soften the crumb, are spread with this mixture. A final sprinkle of olive oil and the "pane oliva" is ready to serve as an appetizer or snack.

SALVATORE MANCINI—PHOTOGRAPHER OF ITRI/KNIGHTSVILLE

Salvatore Mancini needs no introduction to Itrani. If there is one person who best epitomizes the transplanted Itrani and has successfully maintained the global connection it is Salvatore. He is a figure larger than life. A gifted photographer and documenter of the Itrani experience. It was in Italy in 1977 that Sal, known locally as Rhode Island's Master Photographer, finally received international recognition for his work. _The Balaffi Prize_, Italy's most prestigious recognition of photographic excellence was awarded to him that year. Presented in Turin, _The Balaffi Award_ is Italy's highest national prize for photography. The Balaffi Catalogue, distributed internationally was dedicated to Mancini's lengthy photo essay on Italian migrations to the United States and Canada. In particular, the photographs were of the residents of Itri, Italy interspersed with photographs of the transplanted Itrani; residents of Toronto and of Knightsville, Rhode Island.

Born in Itri on December 22, 1947, he migrated with his family to Rhode Island when he was an infant. He brought with him his culture and traditions of his native land. Mancini spent most of his childhood in the sleepy, tightly knit agricultural town of Knightsville, where he was caught up in the romance of the first-generation Italian making his mark in the new country. In his early adult years, following his graduation from Cranston High School and the Rochester Institute of Technology, his life was dominated by shows, lectures and travel. By 1973, he had traveled the United States twice, been to Mexico and spent time in Hawaii. In those days he worked with a 4 x 5 view camera and photographed landscapes and what he calls "photo-therapy" ("photos of myself, acting out ideas before the camera", he explains). Out of his experiences came his first book entitled _Photographs and Poems_, published by Worm Publications in Colorado.

When, at he age of 26 he began to explore his Italian heritage, he began the work that has probably brought him the most satisfaction—his Itri series. In this series, he documented the Itrani experience. Traveling to Toronto, he lived with and photographed the large Itrani community that has settled in Canada. He discovered intriguing parallels between his own life experiences in Knightsville and Cranston and the lives of the Canadian Itrani. Everything from lifestyle to architecture reflected the same cultural influences and traditions that had been transplanted along with the immigrants. Intrigued, he began what has become a journey into his own life. Desiring a place to work surrounded by his subjects, he returned to Itri and rented a house, living there for a year and a half, re-establishing connections while photographing the local scene. At the same time, he began to exhibit his work throughout Italy. Shows in Formia, Casserta, and Siena brought his work to many interested and appreciative Italians. Travels through northern Europe in 1975 expanded Sal's exposure in to Greece and France. A traveling exhibition sponsored by the International Photography Symposium in Arles, France and exhibitions and publications in Rome brought further exposure to his work. Along with the exposure came European recognition. His reputation both as a photographer and artist spread rapidly and he was much in demand.

The second half of the Itrani project involved the return to Knights-ville to photograph the migrated Itrani. He was awarded a grant from the Rhode Island Bicentennial Commission and an exhibit of his work was presented in a one man show in Providence. The show was entitled "*The Passing of The Madonna*," and centered on the religious feast celebrated by Itrani in Italy and simultaneously in America. The final exhibit displayed at the Tonoff Gallery in 1976 was a success. During a return visit to Itri, there was an exhibit of the Itri work, which was the highlight of a magazine article. As a result, he was awarded *The Bolaffi Prize*, the equivalent of being Photographer of the Year.

When he returned to the States in 1977, Mancini approached the Rhode Island Committee for the Humanities with his work. The Committee helped him work out a proposal which ultimately became a film, "*The Americanization of Itri.*" This film chronicles the people of his native town of Itri, and those who immigrated to America and settled in Knights-ville. Important personal testimonies make this film a major contribution to the works on Italian migration. In heartwarming honesty, Itrani speak of conditions in Italy prior to their migration and conditions in America when they arrived. They told of the work conditions of the first years, and of their search for a better life. In the final analysis, the experiences of the Itrani appear to be every immigrant's experience. In the film, Sal relates that the film is a consequence of his return visit to his native village after a twenty year absence he says, "It was as though I had never left. A re-awakening of feelings and memories of my younger self rushed in." In depicting the feast, Mancini juxtaposes the religious feast of the Madonna in Itri with the simultaneously occurring celebration in Knightsville, cleverly showing the cultural unity that exists between the two. As for the success of the Itrani, Sal says, "I think that these first Itrani were fortunate to have settled in Knightsville. They found an agricultural environment very much like they left in Itri. Because of this they were able to utilize their skills immediately and within the first generation they were able to acquire property, establish businesses and educate themselves. Those who settled in industrial centers were not so fortunate." The film was shown on Channel 36 in Rhode Island and at Italian American conferences and symposiums.

Although his current work has taken him in a different direction, Sal would like to someday return to his Itri series and photograph the next generation of Itrani in America as well as in Italy.

FRANCESCO A. CANNELLA -
POET OF THE ITRI/KNIGHTSVILLE EXPERIENCE

Francesco Cannella, or Tony as he known to his friends, is one of the few remaining embodiments of the gifted poet. A natural poet, he expresses in his poetry the soul of the Itrani people. Cannella acts as a filter for the unspoken feelings of the Itrani. He has been endowed with certain gifts, most importantly an acute sensitivity to the world around him. He writes of his own personal feelings, but at the same time they are the feelings of the Itrani of Knightsville. He becomes their voice; he proclaims their love, and their anguish, including their nostalgia for what they have left behind. Whether he is writing of the painful parting from the old country; thoughts of those who have been left and perhaps never to see again; facing the struggles and hardships of life in the new world and the hopes and dreams of the immigrant experience; or of the deep love for his mother, he is speaking for those who cannot speak for themselves. Francesco is acting as the mirror that reflects the Itrani experience for all to see.

Francesco Antonio Cannella was born in the year 1930, in "the beautiful town of Itri, Italy". "My wonderful father was Domenico Cannella and my lovely mother was Rosalba Iole (Inchecchi) Cannella", he says. His grandfather Paolo immigrated to the United States in 1910. He spoke highly about his years in America and learned to speak English very well. He impressed on the young Francesco the dream to go to the great land that his grandfather used to describe.

In the year 1944, because of the World War II, Francesco had to stop school and evacuate to the countryside where his family had a beautiful farm. After the war had ended, the family stayed for an additional year at the farm, because their house had been destroyed by the bombs that were falling daily over Itri. After the family built another home in the town, they returned. Since Francesco was a young teen-ager, his father needed his help to work on the farm, so Fancesco couldn't return to school. In his twenties, he and his friends formed a drama club and presented plays in Itri and other towns. He enjoyed acting and even went for screen tests dreaming to come to America as his grandfather did. In 1955, a farm in California was advertising for young people expert in agriculture and he applied. In June 1956, he was on his way to America, "the land that I always dreamed about". He went to California and worked for four months doing farm work. When one of his sisters came to Cranston, Rhode Island she wrote to him to join her there, which she described as a beautiful town with lots of Italian culture and lots of relatives and friends. In October 1956, he arrived in Cranston and met "Lots of relatives that I never knew before and lots of friends from Itri that were like me with the same dreams". He enrolled in night school to learn the English language. While there, he met "a beautiful girl named Maria," who came to America a few months before he did. After several years, they married and had two children, Domenic and Rosalba, both named after his father and mother. Francesco has four grandchildren, which he describes as "the pride and joy of my life." Tony is 73 years old now and writes,

> "Thanks to God and Thank you Maria SS. Della Civita that I had a wonderful job working as a supervisor in a big company that produces hospital devices. I supported my family and am grateful that I was able to work hard and retire comfortably. I love the country that I was born in, but I love very much this country, America the Beautiful, that gave me hospitality and the opportunity for a better life. We should never stop saying Thank you America, you are so generous and so great!"

LA MAMMA
By Francesco A. Cannella
Dedicata a mia Mamma, alla Mamma Dei miei figli, a tutte le Mamme

La Mamma e' come il sole	*The mother is like the sun*
Ci da' luce e ci riscalda il cuore	*Gives us light and warmth in our heart*
La Mamma e' come una stella	*The mother is like a star*
Passano gli anni e piu' si fa bella	*more beautiful as time passes*
La Mamma e' come la luna	*The mother is like the moon*
Come lei non ce ne' e' nesuna	*No one is quite like her*
La Mamma e' come una rosa	*The mother is like a rose*
E' sempre bella come una sposa	*Always beautiful like a bride*
La Mamma e' come il grande mare	*The mother is like the big ocean*
Si agita, si calma,	*Sometimes a wave, sometimes calm*
E tutti cerca d'amare	*But everyone seeks her love*
La Mamma e' come il vento	*The mother is like the wind*
Non si ferma nemmeno un momento	*Always in motion, she never stops*
La Mamma e' come un fiore	*The mother is like a flower*
E piena di bellezza e inspira l'amore	*Full of beauty, inspiration and love*
La Mamma e come l'aria che si respira	*The mother is like the air we breathe*
Quanto ci manca la testa ci gira	*When air is missing, our head spins*
La Mamma e' il mondo intero	*The mother is like the entire earth*
Credo che nessuno potra' dire:	*I think that no one can say*
Non e' vero	*This is not the truth*

MOVIES MADE IN ITRI LOCALE

TWO WOMEN (LA CIOCIARA) 1960

Vittorio de Sica (Director)
Cesare Zavattina and Vittorio De Sica (screenplay)

CAST

Sophia Loren (Cesira)	Raf Vallone (Giovanni)
Eleonora Brown (Rosetta)	Jean-Paul Belmondo (Michele)
Renato Salvatori (Floundo)	Carlo Ninchi (Michele's father)
Andrea Checchi (Fascist)	

From the novel by Alberto Moravia

Selected as one of the National Film Board's five best foreign films for 1961, this movie firmly established Sophia Loren as an accomplished dramatic actress. She won the Academy Award (the first such citation given the lead in a foreign-language film) and was voted the Best Foreign Actress by the British Film Academy. Among other honors bestowed were the Best Actress awards from the New York Film Critics and the Cannes Film Festival. Originally, Sophia was slated to play the daughter in this motion picture, with Anna Magnani as her mother.

Based on Alberto Moravia's novel, the screenplay was written by Cesare Zavattini. The story line is of Cesira, who is a strong, proud, resourceful, dignified and earthy woman, whose abiding interest in life is her daughter. She had married a man much older than she, because he represented for her a means to attain a better life in Rome, away from the rural poverty of her native village. She had outlived her husband, survived a loveless marriage and had been able to earn a comfortable living runing a small grocery store. Because Allies were bombing her home town, Cesira decides that she must close her shop and get her thirteen-year-old daughter to safety, out of the city to the hills of her native village. Cesira and Rosetta make their way, first by train and then riding mules and later on foot, and must survive the difficulties of lack of food, crazed monks and brutal soldiers along the way.

Back in what she thinks is the safety of her village; a shy school-teacher (Belmondo) falls in love with her, and her daughter secretly falls in love with him. While he is forced to guide retreating Nazis over the mountains, Moroccan soldiers rape both mother and daughter in the ruins of a church. The dazed girl becomes alienated from her mother but is reconciled after learning that the school teacher had been killed. The two women resolve to struggle on together.

The fundamental theme of this film is survival, the will of ordinary people to hang onto life when all around them is chaos, anarchy, and death—the absurdity of war. It gave Italian-Americans images of life and survival in wartime Italy and caught on in popularity. Much of this film was shot on location in the hills around Itri. In many ways it documented for Itrani- Americans in a land so far away-- what life was like for their friends and relative, their fellow Itrani during World War II.

NON C'E' PACE TRA GLI ULIVI

Raf Vallone (Francesco)   Folco Lulli (Lucia)
Giuseppe DeSantis (Director) Passquale De Santis (Cinematographer)

There is No Peace Under The Olive Tree, was filmed in 1950, on location in the hills of Itri. This film became one of Itri's legends, because it used many of the local residents of Itri as extras. Thus, many Itrani became famous as they were being filmed and later when they saw themselves on the screen. The extras earned 10 lire a day for the filming. Part of the exciting folklore of Itri, were stories about how the "new movie stars" were going to spend their earnings-in particular one extra who was using her earnings to buy a new pair of "scarpetta" in Terracina. This film has particular meaning to me, as my mothers father, my grandfather was one of the extra's in the film. My mother receiving news that this filming had occurred in her home town, kept a careful watch of the New York City newspapers so that she might know where and when it would be showing. One day, she asked me to go with her to a small, artsy theatre in Manhattan. We sat through the entire movie after which she was so disapointed. She had not seen her father as expected. Having never seen my grandfather in person, but seeing photographs of him through the years, I told her I thought I had seen him leading a procession in the film, carrying a banner. We sat through the movie one more time. I will never forget the expressions of joy, her hands on her face in amazement at seeing her father- whom she had last seen 25 years prior, from the railing of a large ship as she was leaving for the new world-- on the big screen in a small theatre in New York City.

The film is based on an actual news item. The story concerns an honest, young, shepherd Francesco who returns home after the war. Unfortunately, he finds himself at war once again against local racketeers. He and his fiance' Lucia are pursued by the local villan Bonfiglio. Bonfiglio steals Francesco's sheep and turns the story around so that Francesco is imprisoned. Good eventually prevails and Bonfiglio is punished. He dies a villans death by falling off of a cliff.

Pasquale De Santis, the Italian cinematographer, photographed, this his first film in collaboration with his older brother, the Director Giuseppe De Santis. Mr. De Santis was born not too far from where he photographed this film, in Fondi in 1927.

CHAPTER 5
ITRANI FOLKLORE

Ever since humans first learned to speak, parents have told stories to their children. Storytelling has the power not only to entertain, but to teach, to heal, and to transmit traditions and family lore from one generation to the next. Whether the legends are well-worn folk tales, family lore, little songs, proverbs, or fantasies invented on the spot, they convey to those who listen a special sense of security and a knowledge of his or her place in the world. These are perhaps the most effective teaching tools ever used. All of the world's cultures use tales and proverbs to preserve and transmit beliefs and values. They can serve as lectures. If a parent wants to make a point without lecturing, a proverb could be used. Sometimes a song or proverb is a healing activity. When a child is hurt or ill, or frustrated and angry, an appropriate proverb can ease the pain. If someone lacks confidence, a story from family folk-lore can deliver the message.

ITRANI PROVERBS

Proverbs are not merely decorations on life. A proverb is a traditional saying which offers advice or presents a moral in a short manner. They have life itself in them. They are the bedrock substance of living, built up by many people and many years. They develop over the years, in every community because of some local custom, local story or local character. Sometimes the story has been forgotten and all that is left is the proverb. In this way, the community has its proverbial characters as well as its proverbs which deliver powerful messages. Local sayings may allude to the character of the place and the people, with jests and gibes about the weather, seasons, landmarks, towns, customs, and similar features. Proverbs may be used to spice up our conversation with traditional formulas we have heard others use in similar contexts. They can sum up the situation we are talking about. Because they are traditional and suggest that generations of experience lie behind them, they are readily accepted. Furthermore, their meaning is immediately understood by others within the context they are used. Proverbs can be used to comment on someone else's behavior or to defend one's own action and attitude. A story from my own family illustrates this point. My Aunt Italia told me a story of my grandmother coming upon some paisani, who she had heard gossiping about her. She turned to them and said, "Mirati allo specchio Che quello te la dice la verita se c'e lai," (Look into the mirror, if you have one. There you will see the truth. Or, another interpretation would be "mirrors don't lie!")

Proverbs fall readily into several categories. Those of the first type are the form of abstract statements expressing general truths, such as; Absence makes the heart grow fonder. Proverbs of the second type take specific observations from everyday experience to make a point which is general, for example: Don't put all your eggs in one basket. The third type of proverb comprises sayings from particular areas of traditional wisdom and folklore. In this category are found the health proverbs such as: Feed a cold and starve a fever. In addition, there are traditional country proverb which relate to husbandry, the seasons, and the weather, such as; Red sky at night, Shepherd's delight; red sky in the morning, shepherd's warning. In general, they represent a folk philosophy.

Itri, as in most cultures, has a tradition of proverbs that express ideas and beliefs commonly held by its people. Several of the more common Itrani proverbs are included here. Attempts to categorize these proverbs in terms of the values they seem to stress reflect the Itrani's emphasis on: the family, friendship, health, caution, planning ahead, and the need to not waste time.

The first proverb I will list is my very favorite and that is probably because I heard it repeatedly from my parents' through-out my growing years. I can still see my mother, arms raised to the sky, in a gesture of exasperation uttering the following proverb:

Un padre puo mantenere centi figli, ma centi figli non
se capace di mantenere un padre.

(A father can support one hundred children, but one hundred children cannot support one father)

PROVERBS OF FRIENDHIPS

Una amica vale un tesora

(A good friend is worth more than treasure)

Amici di tutti, amici di nessuno

(A friend to all is a friend to none)

Oggi tu, e domani le mei

(Your turn today, mine tomorrow)

La migliore parola e' quella che non si dice

(The best word is that which is not spoken)

Amico e vino vogliono essere vecchi

(Friends and wine should be old)

PROVERBS ABOUT WORK

Che mangia a carnevale, E paga a Pasqua

Fa buona carnevale, E mala Pasqua

(Who eats at carnevalle and pays on Easter, has a good carnevalle and a bad Easter)

Pulisht la casa, non sai chi ce tras

(Keep your house clean, you never know who will enter)

Fatt lu liet, non sai che aspetti

(Make your bed, you never know who it awaits)

Chi va al mulino s'u farina

(He who goes to the mill, gets the flour)

Chi' cucina in temp, mangia a ora

(He who cooks in time, eats in time)

Chi dorme non piglia pesci

(He who sleeps does not catch fish)

Batti le fierri quando e caldo

(Strike while the iron is hot)

PROVERBS OF LIFE PHILOSOPHY

Lavara la testa al'asino e' perdere l'acqua e il sapone

(Wash a jackass's head, and you are sure to lose both soap and water)

Il cane che abbaia, non fa la caccia

(The dog that barks, is not a hunting dog)

Bandiera vecchia onore di capitano
   (An old flag is an honor to the captain)
Tu po porte l'assine a fontana, no poi forzare a bere
   *(You can lead a donkey to the fountain, but you can't force him
to drink)*
Chi nasce tondo, non muore quadrato
   (He who is born round, does not die square)
Aiutati che Dio Ti Aiuta
   (God helps those who help themselves)
Solo alla morte non c'e rimedio
   (Only death has no remedy)
Chi va paino va sano e va longano
   (He who proceeds slowly, goes both safely and further)
Misurati al buco prima che entri
   (Measure that hole before you enter it)
Chi ha la salute e' ricco
   (He who has health has wealth)
Chi risica, rosica
   (Nothing ventured, nothing gained)
Anche le mure hanno l'orrechi
   (Even the walls have ears)
Mezzo pani e' meglia di nienti
   (Half a loaf is better than none)

Looking at these proverbs in terms of the values they stress empha-
sizes how this folklore genre can reflect a group's ethos. These examples
do not entirely exhaust the Itrani proverbial lore, but they do suggest the
ways in which the general values and attitudes of a culture can be derived
from looking at its proverbial lore. But proverbs take their richest depths
of meaning within the context of actual usage when someone recognizes
their applicability to a particular situation. For example, one of our family
stories includes one told by Nonno Stefano. When a paisano in Itri heard
that my Aunt Italia was getting married he stopped to congratulate my
grandfather. The text of the greeting was that finally my aunt, who was
36 years old, was getting married. Nonno Stefano replied:

Quando la pere e mattura cade sole
   (When the pear is ripe it falls by itself)

Thus, the art of proverb use lies not so much in memorizing them, but from the ability to select the appropriate traditional idea for the specific occasion. In every case, the proverb represents the force of a community opinion that has been honed by generations of experience. Using and heeding proverbs allows one to follow the advice of generations of predecessors.

FOLK SONGS

Music occupies a conspicuous place in the life of the Itrani. The folk songs are the favorites. The holiday seasons find families joining in singing Itrani folk songs to the accompaniment of mandolin or guitar. No wedding, christening or other celebration is complete without this folk music. Some of the older Itrani know dozens of the songs and are frequently called upon for their own renditions. The folk music tradition, homespun and rural fit into the Itrani pattern of neighborly work and useful pleasure. Wherever the Itrani went, he carried with him the old-time songs and the old-time singing that reflected his life. To teach others everywhere the art of singing Itrani folk songs, was not only for enjoyment and entertainment but also for prayer.

The two outstanding types of folk songs are the Itrani melodies and the Stornelli Romani. The former are sung during work and play times and have a theme, being of either love or sacrifice. The words of the Stornelli, which has a constant tune, are made up by two singers as they go along. Stornelli can frequently take on an insulting character which is traditional and done in fun. These songs are an important medium of folk song transmissions. For folk song lives not by the oral tradition alone; the folk memory preserved is carefully compiled and treasured. They help to diffuse, as well as to re-create the tradition of the culture.

The following are a series of songs that were narrated to me by my Aunt Italia a native of Itri, who immigrated to the United States in 1953 and is currently 88 years old.

Luccellino dal mare

Luccelino che viene dal mare
Che viene ci due che
Vinene a fare
Sul tuo balcone
Vinene a pasare
Un mazzolino di fioure per te

Piove

Piove, esche il sole
La Madonna prende un fiore
Prende un fiore per Gesu
E Domani no piove pui

School Song (1920)

Sul Colle libero!
Questo coraggio
Passe passagio
E viva la scuola
E viva il lavore

Luccelleto

Quando viene luccelleto
Porto un foglio sui piedi
Un saluto un bigletto
Alla mama per te

San Pasquale—(A prayer recited by one seeking a spouse)

San Pasquale Bailon
Prodettore delle donne
Famma trovare una bel'marito
Bianchi, Rosso, e colorito
Come Voi, ma tale e quale,
O glorioso San Pasquale

Courtship Song Amore D'ammi Quel Falzolettino

Amore dammi quel falzolettino

Che vado allo fondo e lo vado a lava

Te lo lava e te lo lavo e te lo rischiaro

Te lo lavo e te lo rischiaro e le to stento sul ramo d'un fior

Ti lo stendo sul ramo d'un fiore

Te es stendo sul ramo di fiore vento

D'amore l'asciughera

Te lo stiro col ferro a vapore'

Te lo stiro col ferro a vaporre ed ogni stimata un bacino d'amor!

Canzonetta Di Mio Nonno—Michelangelo Fabrizio
By Italia Fabrizio Sinapi

Sant'Angelo di Dio la notte viene

Qiu a riposare vado zo'e meco vinei tua

A te mio caro amico, con voti e riverenza

Alla vostra obbedienza Io mi soggetto

Fate che nel mio petto, ardid'amor Celeste

Consuma ogni peste di peccato

Mi raccomanto a Re, to spiroto del ciel

Che scacci tu da me e, l'ocifero crudele

Difendiui per pieta, questamma assai di piu

E quanto poi sara

Consequela a Gesu

Some other Local Songs

I

Bella ci so' venuto pe' sapere

Se c'e' principio de poterci amare,

Se c'e' principio. Fammelo sapere,

Se no, da te me vogio alontanare.

II

Site piu' iauta (alta) vuje che la chenna (canna)

La fragranza tenite de gliu' rosmarino,

Tenite la bellezza di Sent'Enna (Sant' Anna)

E gli begli uocchi di Senta Lucia;

Tenite le manuzze di Sen Giuenne (San Giovanni),
Gliu personale di Madre Maria
III
Giovane fresca, vaga e 'nnamorata,
Seria, pura, gentile, onesta e bella,
Pari 'mparadiso fabbricata.
Ciascuno dei tuoi belli occhi pare stella,
La fronte spaziosa e 'l capo d'oro,
Che vale piu d'ogni altro gran tesoro

FOLK SAY – WORD LORE THE USE OF NICKNAMES – SOPRANOMMO

For another kind of folk tradition involving speech, we turn to the odd custom among the Itrani of bestowing nicknames on one another—not in the spirit of levity, but in dead earnest—so earnestly, in fact, that the nickname replaces the surname of entire families. Some of these nicknames have been in use so long that, in the course of generations the real family names have become obscured. In fact, it is common knowledge that the mailman in Itri couldn't deliver the mail unless he knew the nicknames of all of its residents.

Sometimes it is simply that the smallness of rural communities and the familiarity of all the members with one another precluded the need for surnames. Patronymics in Italy first came into use during the Napoleonic era as a result of French officials discovering the lack of surnames. These bureaucrats arbitrarily assigned to each family the name of its home town or some other descriptive and identifying word. Because of the size of families, for example, Maria Civita might yet mean several different women. This is particularly true in Itri, where Maria or Civita or Maria Civita was a favorite name for female babies, being named after the patron saint of Itri.

The nicknames record traits or characteristics both personal and professional. Sometimes they are complimentary, and again they are intended to satirize, or caricature those to whom they are given. No name is too sacred or too base for them to shorten or modify into an affectionate, humorous, or abusive sobrequet. The butcher, for example, might become Jack the Butcher, and his son, Jack the Butcher's son

Tony. They might be affectionate or deprecatory. At times the nicknames might be unflattering and constitute insults. A woman who is disorderly in her appearance might draw the unkindly label, La Zuzusa, a dialect word meaning "dirty." The author, Richard Gambino recalled a woman in his Brooklyn neighborhood known only as La Sporca (The Dirty One) because of her unkempt appearance. On the other hand, they might be affectionate as was the nickname given to my daughter who was born with red hair, -- "Caporossa", or an attractive female neighbor might be called "Luisa, pezzo di pasta" (Luisa, that piece of pastry). My own grandfather on my father's side was known as "Papa duLuc"—my mother's father was known as "Stefano de Cavour" after a military hero named Camillo Benzo Conte di Cavour.

Sopranommo's are an insight into the historical development of towns and cities; into humorous civic and personal struggles, or into the commercial and social development of these places. The classes of sopranommos range from the most ordinary objects of life to complex religious and political organizations. They may be interwoven with the biographies and accomplishments of these persons. It is instructive and often amusing to note the vast number of nicknames and see how they reflect an attempt to berate or to elevate the individual.

To illustrate the use of nicknames among the Itrani, the following is a transcript of a tape, which was presented to a newly married couple, describing their wedding ceremony and reception party using the guests' sopranommos.

• •

MATRIMONIA ITRANO
Chiese de Sant Angelo
Giorno di Nozze
14, Aprile, 1979

SPOSI	**COMPARE E COMMARE**
Felice de Cazzigli	Guiseppe de Cazzone d'anello
Maria Zipinculo	Marianina Putanella

Le Destimonio

Cicciglio Dinculo	Francesca Pane e' Oglio
Pasquale Ottipalle	Terese Curo Sicco

Faggetto (Damigella d'onore)

Uotto di Pantano
Notaio Rogatone
Broglitto

The marriage was conducted by **SACERDOTE (The Priest)**
Il figlio di Pisciaturo (The Fisherman's Son)

Invitati: (Invited guests)

Cacaiaglio	Straccia Zoccole
Caca Allupiatt	Maronna Maddumane
Pizza la Merd	Cap de Fierr
Gesu Christo	Santu Tiaur
Patatern	Piscia Fiene
In Fregna La Mort	Spoglia Maronna

Invitati, continued:

Cauzone	Ficchione	Rughetti
Piscia Nobile	Ciuettale	Scoccia Canale
Scatulell	Magnione	Mulite
Mangia Cane	Zannone	Rulite
Puzza Fiato	Giu Cane	Ospranghel
Pane e' Farnio	Capretto	Stracciuleil
Cardiglia	Pasta e' Cici	Carusiel
Soto Acit	La Stortio	Ciardugl
Cap de Case	Orsulini	Fica Secce
Pasta e' Fasul	Tira Tira	Cacacca
Martinelli	Fabiane	Ficuocco
Vacazza	Lu Scacat	La Zuoppo
Zumbariel	Tatoline	Sette Malizie
Tutliell	La Piattare	Suot Cuot
Caccia la Merd	La Frange	Ciocirelle

| Lu Cinciare | Zampacort | La Monachelle |
| Pistole | Cap de Puorch | Pane e' Oglio |

Dopo la ceremonia tutte alle Ristorante Monte Fusco
(After the church ceremony everyone met for the wedding dinner
at Monte Fusco Restaurant)

Even the Chef's were Itrani:

Chefs
Antonio Iattamorta   Maria Magnicani

Camiere (the waiters)
Teresa Ciciurind	Marianina di Cicoria
Giuannina La Sorda	Anna Scacciarina
Teresa Pizzancuolo	Antoinette la Capretta

TAVOLO D'ONORE: (The table of honor)
SPOSO-The Grooms's Table of Honor
Gesu Cristo	Patatern	Santutiaur
Spoglia Maronna	Maronna Maddumane	
In Fregna La Mort		
La Famiglia de Puttanella		

LA SPOSA (The Bride's Table of Honor)
| Caccia Merdi | Caca Lai Piatte | Pisciature |
| Pizza La Merda | Caca Sotti | Casotto |

RITARDATARI (The late arrivals)
Ricchione	Santumartini	La Croce
Munsignore	Piez de Pizz	Canducc de Pane
Un Bastore Vacche	Tamburrine	Capo Russo
Pecora Cotta		

META DI PRANZA—I BRINDISI

(During the dinner, the toasts to the happy couple begin)

Gesu Cristo is the first to toast:

"Questo vino e' bello e' fino

Alle saluti dei sposi di questa mattina."

(The guests applaud the toast as the bride and groom kiss.)

Putanella stands up and toasts:

"Questo vino e Rosso e secco

Alla saluti della famiglia fice secca"

Ciccurinda toasts the bride and groom with the following
brindisi:

"Questo vino non e fatto col bastona

Alla saluti della famiglia di Pistola"

A toast follows by Zia Italia:

"Questo vino e bello e' calante

Alla saluti di tutti quanti"

Another toast was offered by Puttanella:

"Questo vino e' rosso e' chiaro

Alla salute di tutti Li Itrani"

IL PRANZO PROSECUIVA –(The dinner proceeds. There were
some guests who ate lots of food. They were called the
"**MANGIONE**") These were identified as:

Magnone	Ruscone	Mangia Cane
Zannone	I Uott di Padane	

A FINI PRANZA--COMINCINO DANZA

(After the dinner, the dancing began)

The first to get up to dance were:

Zumbarriell	La Stuort	La Zuopi
Zambucort	Zump Aglu Fuoss	

Everyone applauds the dancers with more toasts:

"E Viva Lu Stuort"

"E Viva Zuopi!"

Capo Rosso leads the invited guests in a final toast to the bride and groom as they are leaving the restaurant to begin their new life together:

"Cent'anni e figli maschi"

CONCLUSION

The flags of both America and Italy fly side by side above the entrance of a restaurant on Cranston Street in Knightsville. The owners of the caffe, Greg Spremulli and Joe DeQuattro, both descendants of Itrani immigrants decided to pursue a mutual interest, cooking and serving the authentic foods of the Itrani culture. They enrolled in culinary and pastry schools and integrated their childhood memories of fresh, regional foods with the lessons learned in school. They then opened their own restaurant in Knightsville, **_Caffe' Itri_**. One look at the menu and the customer sees that Greg and Joe have maintained the traditional "old style" of cooking. The restaurant offers traditional "peasant dishes" such as escarole sauteed in cannellini beans; or frizella-tomato and basil salad with fresh mozzarella on top of toasted bread: wood-grilled Veal; grilled Pizza, stuffed artichokes and homemade Pastas. They take pride in providing their customers with the highest-quality food, steeped in old-world tradition and strive to

MY GRANDFATHER CAVALIERE STEFANO FABRIZIO

111

MEDALS AWARDED WITH "CAVALIERIE AWARD"

keep the Itrani traditions alive for generations to come. Although, winners of many awards, the one that Greg and Joe are most proud of was when **_Caffe Itri_** was voted "The Best Italian Food in Rhode Island" by Rhode Island Monthly Magazine in August 1995.

The flavor of the Itrani heritage and culture remains strong in Knightsville. Knightsville is still home to many of the original families that immigrated to Rhode Island and stayed. The original immigrants although poor, uneducated and superstitious were in possession of a strong courage. They brought with them a spirit of joy and curiosity, a willingness to work hard, to take the good with the bad, and to prosper and grow in their new country. Out of the immigrant emerges a third generation and the fruition of the slow process of assimilation can be seen. The members of this generation are industrious, intelligent, educated, and motivated by the same drive that their ancestors had. They can be found in the professions as doctors, architects, engineers, lawyers and judges, teachers, politicians, businessmen, and as Greg and Joe, restaurateurs.

There is a new awakening among Itrani. The grandchildren and great-grandchildren of the immigrants are becoming interested in learning more about whom they are and where their grandparents came from. The study of the Italian language is gaining new popularity. Many of the more affluent Itrani have left the old neighborhoods, only to return to the place of their childhood in later years to re-discover their heritage. Despite the trend towards assimilation, there remain many visible examples of Itrani presence in Knightsville. The Itrani dialect is still spoken. One can still buy fruits and vegetables raised by the descendants of those early pioneers from Itri. Most live in modest homes with immaculately kept gardens. There you can find herbs such as parsley, fresh oregano, arrugula, tomatoes and other vegetables lovingly cultivated and harvested. Also, there is inevitably the traditional grape arbor that will be gently cared for in the expectation of the fall harvest that will provide for the family that wonderful home made wine. The pride of their heritage is reflected in one of the most active Italian service organizations that continue to service in charitable and civic affairs. But more importantly, the Itrani maintained the religious festival that is the core of their collective identity: the annual feast of the Madonna Della Civita, the patron saint of Itri. The feast in July attracts hundreds of second

and third generation Itrani, as well as non-Italians who appreciate the celebration and the fine food that is offered. The canopied booths are still there bulging with pizza, sausage-and-eggplant sandwiches, zeppolo, lemon ices, torrone, nuts, funnel cakes, balloons, dolls, hats, and games of chance. Itrani from Italy are still coming to Knightsville, and Knightsville Itrani are still visiting their home town, Itri during feast time. The feeling of dual loyalty to both America and Italy has been very strong with most Itrani. For this reason, Itrani immigrants never completely lost their ties with the old world and never really wanted to lose these ties.

"CAVALIERE AWARD" GIVEN TO MY GRANDFATHER STEFANO FABRIZIO IN 1920. THIS AWARD IS THE ITALIAN EQUIVALENT OF ENGLAND'S KNIGHTHOOD. COURTESY OF GRANDSON STEFANO FABRIZIO

BIBLIOGRAPHIC NOTE:

The historical materials presented in this work were obtained through oral interviews with members of the Italian community of Itri, in Italy and the Italian American community of Knightsville in Rhode Island. The following textual references were also consulted and cited.

Alba, Richard. *Italian-Americans: Into the Twilight of Ethnicity*. Englewood Cliffs, New Jersey: Prentice-Hall. 1985.

Amfitheatrof, Erik. *The Children of Columbus: An Informal History of the Italians in the New World*. Boston: Little Brown, 1973.

Bailey, Samuel L. *"The Adjustment of Italian Immigrants in Buenos Aires and New York, 1870-1914."* American Historical Review, 1983.

Bardaglio, Peter W. *Italian Immigrants and the Catholic Church in Providence, 1890- 1930. Rhode Island*, The Rhode Island Historical Society, 1975.

Battistella, Graziano, Italian Americans in the 80's: A Sociodemographic Profile, Center for Migration Studies, New York. 1989. P.10.

Bianco, Carla, *The Two Rosetos*. Bloomington: Indiana University Press, 1974.

Bureau of The Census, *Historical Statistics of The United States, Colonial Times to 1970*, Washington, D.C.: U.S. Government Printing Office.

Bureau of The Census, *Compendium of the United States Census*, Washington, 1990.

Coleman, Peter J. *The Transformation of Rhode Island, 1790-1860*. Brown University Press, Providence, 1969.

Cranston News, Cranston Rhode Island, July 20, 1927.

Cranston Historical Society, Cranston Rhode Island.

Dinnerstein, Leonard. *The Aliens: A History of Ethnic Minorities in America*. New York: Appleton-Century-Crofts, 1970.

Echo, The, Joe Fuoco, Editor, *The Echo Publishing Company*, July 10-24, 1992, January 5, 1998.

Gallo, Patrick, *Ethnic Alienation: The Italian-Americans*. Rutherford, New Jersey: Farleigh Dickinson, 1974.

Gambino, Richard. *Blood of My Blood: The Dilemma of The Italian Americans* Garden City, New York Doubleday, 1974.

Hewitt, W. Phil, *The Italian Texans*, The University of Texas, San Antonio, 1973.

Jordan, P, *"The Sons and Daughters of Itri"*, Yankee Magazine, March 1993.

Juliani, Richard. *Family and Community Life of Italian Americans*, 1971.

Lazio, M. *Invito Al Folclore*, Instituto Geografico De Agostini, Novara, Italy, 1984.

Lepis, Louis A. *Italian Heroes of American History*, Americans of Italian Descent, Inc. New York, 1976.

LoGatto, Anthony F. *The Italians in America, 1492-1972*. Ocean Park, New York 1972.

MacDonald, John and Beatrice MacDonald. *"Chain Migration, Ethnic Neighborhood Formation, and Social Networks,"* Millbank Memorial Fund Quarterly, January, 1964, 1970.

McLaughlin, William G. *Rhode Island: A History*, W.W. Norton & Co, Inc. New York, 1978.

Mancini, Salvatore, *"The Americanization of Itri"*. Video produced by Salvatore Mancini.

Monahan, Clifford P. *Rhode Island, A student's Guide To Localized History*, Teachers College Press, New York 1965.

Nelli, Humbert S. *The Italians in Chicago, 1880-1930: A Study in Ethnic Mobility*. New York: Oxford University Press, 1970.

Pisani, Lawrence, *The Italians In America: A Social Study and History.* New York, 1957.

Print-It, *Cranston Print Works Company*, Vol. 2, Issue No. 7, July, 1947.

Providence Journal, Providence, Rhode Island. Sunday, October 7, 1888.

Rhode Island Manual, Ocean State *Governors, Under the Constitution.*

Riis, Jacob, "*Feast* Days in Little Italy," The Century Magazine, 1899.

Rose, Philip M. *The Italians in America*, New York: George H. Doran, 1922.

Santoro, Carmela E. *The Italians in Rhode Island: The Age of Exploration to the Present*, 1524-1989, The Rhode Island Publications Society and The Rhode Island Heritage Commission, Providence, 1990.

Sartorio, Enrico Charles, *Social and Religious Life of Italians in America*, Augustus M. Kelley, Clifton, 1974.

Schiavo, Giovanni, *Italian American History: The Italian Contribution to The Catholic Church in America*, New York, Arno Press. 1975.

Smith, Judith E, *A History of Italians & Jewish Immigrant Lives in Providence, Rhode Island, 1900-1940.* State University of New York Press, Albany, 1985.

St. Mary's Feast Society Annual Banquet Journal, April 27, 1991.

Trevelyn, Raleigh. *Rome"44: The Battle For The Eternal City*, The Viking Press, New York, 1981.

Tricarico, Donald. "*The Restructuring of Ethnic Community: The Italian Neighborhood In Greenwich Village*," Journal of Ethnic Studies 11. no. 2 (1983).

U.S. Census Bureau, 2001, *Profile of Selected Social Characteristics: 2000.* Census 2000 Supplementary Survey Summary Tables, Washington, D.C.: U.S. Government Printing Office.

Walters, Gordon. Magill's *Survey of Cinema*, 1987

Vecoli, Rudolph J., *Introduction to Italian Immigrants in Rural and Small Town America.* Essays from the Fourteenth Annual Conference of the American Italian Historical Association, ed. Rudolph J. Vecoli, (Staten Island, New York) 1979

LIBRARY EXHIBIT

The American Italian Historical Association-Long Island Regional Chapter and The Farmingdale Public Library will present a new exhibition, "From Italy to Rhode Island—the migration of the Itrani to America". The exhibit, a collection of photographs and artifacts is being presented in celebration of Italian Heritage Month and will be at the Library through October 31st, in the lower exhibition hall. The exhibit was assembled by Dr. Anne T. Romano, President of the Long Island Regional Chapter of The A.I.H.A. She will give a talk at the Library about the exhibit on Monday, October 3rd, at 6 p.m.

This exhibit, From Italy to Rhode Island is the culmination of more than 15 years of work by Dr. Romano, whose primary subjects are the Itrani, those immigrants from a litle village in Italy, between Naples and Rome. The Itrani emigrated to another small village in Cranston, Rhode Island called Knightsville. The photographs illuminate the continued exploration of the relationships between Italy and America, and the Italian American culture. It also illuminates the importance of family, culture, and religion to the early immigrants and the role they play for the children of immigrants today.

The Farmingdale Public Library is open Monday through Sunday from 10:00a.m. to 6:00 p.m. For further information, or travel directions, visit:

www.farmingdale library.edu.

Printed in the United States
219306BV00003B/1/A